SIMPLY FAULKNER

SIMPLY FAULKNER

PHILIP WEINSTEIN

Simply Charly

New York

Simply Charly
5 Columbus Circle, 8th Fl
New York, NY 10019
www.simplycharly.com

ISBN: 978-1-943657-07-0

For Penny

Contents

Praise for *Simply Faulkner*

"As Philip Weinstein suggests, there is no better way to begin than by plunging into the work of William Faulkner. But it's immensely useful to have at one's elbow a knowledgeable guide, and there is none better than Weinstein. He himself is a brilliant writer—clear, concrete, smart, suggestive—and this short book represents an ideal introduction to the major work of America's most important modern author. I would strongly recommend this book to anyone interested in Faulkner."

—**Jay Parini, author of** *One Matchless Time: A Life of William Faulkner* **and** *Empire of Self: A Life of Gore Vidal*

"Philip Weinstein's newest book on William Faulkner offers a rich, compact discussion of Faulkner's life and work that will engage both new readers and those who are familiar with the writing of the most important novelist of 20th century America. Clarity and penetrating insight are combined in *Simply Faulkner* to move through Faulkner's complexity in order to discern the specificities and magnitude of his achievement. This is a book for every reader of Faulkner's fiction."

—**Patrick O'Donnell, Professor of Twentieth and Twenty-First Century British and American Literature, Michigan State University**

"Philip Weinstein's concise Faulkner biography is a wonder of compression and interpretation of the Mississippi writer's creative life. It demonstrates the fruits of the author's career-long devotion to insightful readings of Faulkner's works. Weinstein's well-deserved reputation as a scholar, critic, and excellent writer is manifest on every page."

—**Thomas McHaney, Kenneth M. England Professor of Southern Literature Emeritus, Georgia State University**

"A brilliant selection of revealing vignettes from Faulkner's life and work, opening long views into both his achievements and his limitations, the writing of both his own and his culture's 'hemorrhaging.'"

—**Richard Moreland, Louisiana State University, author** of *Faulkner and Modernism*

"One of the most insightful William Faulkner scholars, Philip Weinstein shares with readers, in plain language, his deep expertise in the modernist writer's life and work. Weinstein's insights into Faulkner's background, his attitude toward the 'cauldron of race and class tension' in the South, his love and social life, as well as his personal struggles, helps ease the way, for readers new and old, toward a clearer understanding of Faulkner."

—**Jacques Pothier, Professor of North American Literature, Université de Versailles Saint-Quentin-en-Yvelines**

"Boiling down the tumultuous life, prolific career, intense vision, and dazzling aesthetic of one of the twentieth century's most audacious literary figures to a hundred pages is a seemingly impossible task. But Philip Weinstein has done it. Here is one of William Faulkner's finest critics at his luminous, provocative best. With its deep insights and crisp prose, *Simply Faulkner* is anything but."

—**Jay Watson, Howry Professor of Faulkner Studies and Professor of English at the University of Mississippi**

Other *Great Lives* Titles

Series Editor's Foreword

Simply Charly's *Great Lives Series* offers brief, but authoritative, biographies of the world's most influential people—scientists, artists, writers, economists, and other historical figures whose contributions have had a meaningful and enduring impact on our society. Each book, presented in an engaging and accessible fashion, offers an illuminating look at their works, ideas, personal lives, and the legacies they left behind.

Our authors are prominent scholars and other top experts who have dedicated their careers to exploring each facet of their subjects' work and personal lives.

Unlike many other biographies that are simply descriptions of the major milestones in a person's life, the *Great Lives Series* goes above and beyond the standard format to include not just the facts, but also fascinating information about the little-known character traits, quirks, strengths and frailties that had shaped these extraordinary individuals' lives and, consequently, their professional achievements.

Whether shrouded in secrecy, surrounded by myths and misconceptions, or caught up in controversies, the *Great Lives Series* brings substance, depth, and clarity to the sometimes-complex lives of history's most powerful and influential people.

What can a reader learn from the *Great Lives Series?* The books relate how each person's family, childhood, formative years, and later relationships had influenced their adult lives and career paths. The volumes also shed light on the thought process that led these remarkable people to their groundbreaking discoveries or other achievements, as well as the challenges they had to face and overcome to make history in their respective fields.

We hope that by exploring these biographies, readers will not only gain new knowledge and understanding of what drove these geniuses, but also find inspiration for their own lives. Isn't this what a great book is supposed to do?

Charles Carlini, Simply Charly
New York City

Preface

Let's begin by acknowledging that *Simply Faulkner* does not imply a *simple* Faulkner. The word "simply" runs the gamut of meanings—from "merely" or "only," to "really" or "completely." This book aspires to the latter sense of "simply" by attempting to show in plain words why the works of this Nobel Prize-winning American novelist matter.

Why must *Simply Faulkner* refuse the appeal of a simple Faulkner? Even those who press this question may suspect that a "simple Faulkner" is a contradiction in terms. It is not just that his life was messy—complicated by recurrent pretentions as to who he was and what he did—but also because it was marked by lifelong solitariness, marital problems, family disasters, and abiding alcoholism. But the more important point is that Faulkner's work is fundamentally *un*simple. I found this out when I first attempted to read one of Faulkner's works while a senior at a decent Southern high school. I tried four times to get through *Absalom, Absalom!*. But I failed each time to get past the first chapter, and—humiliated and filled with rage—I threw the book on the floor. I did not try to read him again until three years later. Faulkner's great work is convoluted, and its narrative procedures are unfamiliar. If you are a general reader attempting to make your way through one of his masterpieces, you are likely to think that you don't know how to read this book. You cannot get its sentences to work for you and cannot grasp the logic of its sequences. You may well think that your inability to comprehend Faulkner's writing is his fault. After all, how dare he make you feel that you no longer know how to read a novel? But that is precisely the nature of Faulkner's best work: he refuses to herd his prose through the familiar hoops of syntax and sequence—of grammatically well-bred sentences—that we recognize as the building blocks of novels. Instead, he writes as though most novels are to him a waste of time. Moreover, the trouble he seems to find with these works is foundational; it lodges in the nature of words themselves and in the novelistic conventions that writers draw on for stringing words together—"just a shape to fill a lack," as one of his memorable characters, Addie Bundren, thinks of words in *As I Lay Dying*. To her, words are a failed substitute for nonverbal experience: "That was when I learned that words are no good; that words don't ever fit even what they are trying to say at . . . that fear was invented by someone that had never had the fear; pride, who never had the pride." Words, Addie concludes, "go straight up in a thin line" while "doing goes along the earth, clinging to it," speechlessly.

Before dismissing this conviction as nonsense, try to remember a moment when you had something urgent to say, and you became aware that language was failing you—perhaps when you struggled to tell someone what you actually felt and thought when you lost your job, when your first child was born, when you fell in love, or when your father died. At such intense moments we are nearest to recognizing that the words are . . . just words. The realm they operate in is language; it is not life. The experience you were trying to express was something entirely different—overpowering yet wordless. The words feebly point to what they cannot say.

If you believed that words mainly betray the experience they pretend to convey, you would either not write novels at all or at least not write conventional ones. If you persevered in writing anyway, you would find yourself in an endless struggle with words themselves, trying to keep them from going "straight up in a thin line," as Addie put it. Instead, you would labor to trick them into saying life as it actually happens: as doings that occur speechlessly, "along the earth." This is the central reason for Faulkner's difficulty. Novels that too easily turn the messiness of life into the orderliness of words are—for him—like CliffsNotes substituting for the actual complexity of the

real thing: oversimplified, too neat and regulated, their o
superficially pleasing but ultimately weightless. The verbal rep
give on nonverbal reality is inauthentic.

To this intrinsic reason for Faulkner's difficulty—lodged in his
quarrel with the medium itself—we may add others. All of these are
external to the treachery lurking in language as such. Let's look at
Faulkner in the context of his times. Born in Mississippi in 1897,
he came of age in the second decade of the 20th century. Like so
many writers of that era, he was deeply marked by the Great War
of 1914-1918. Faulkner never fought in WWI (though he stoutly
pretended otherwise), yet its shadow haunted his life and penetrated
his dreams. "The Jerries are after me!" his terrified mistress, Meta
Carpenter, remembered a nightmare-ridden Faulkner screaming in his
sleep early one morning. This was some 20 years after the war had
ended. He who had seen no action over France was somehow a war
victim nevertheless.

It was, moreover, a war that did not make sense. Heads of state
were never able to explain persuasively why it had to be fought. World
War I seemed more like an absurd affair of political jockeying than
a cataclysm driven by any country's existential interest. Nor did it
proceed as earlier wars had. There were no decisive battles; a hill or
valley taken by the Allies from the Germans (at great human cost)
would be re-occupied by the Germans (again, at great human cost)
soon after. The waiting was almost as bad as the fighting. Coffin-like
trenches were repeatedly soaked with rain, filth, and blood. ("I think
we are in rats' alley/ Where the dead men lost their bones," so had poet
T. S. Eliot alluded to trench realities in *The Waste Land* [1922]).

Worse, the death-dealing apparatus unleashed in that war—the
newly invented machine guns and the insidious mustard
gas—outflanked each army's resources. And there were mental and
emotional scars as well; men who came home from the front often
suffered from shell shock—as the reaction to the trauma of battle
became known. This previously unknown condition demonstrated
that the brutality of such a war could register as an unbearable assault
on the human mind and senses. Many of the wounded soldiers were

incapable of dealing with such trauma, often resulting in a psychological meltdown.

It is therefore no accident that the writers of the 1920s and 1930s—Faulkner and Eliot, but also Ezra Pound, James Joyce, Gertrude Stein, John Dos Passos and Ernest Hemingway, to list just a few—saw World War I as a bankrupting of the 19th century values by which they—and others—had made sense of life. For them, it was no longer possible to write literature under the banner of "Civility" and "Significance." In 1923, Eliot published a widely-read review of Joyce's *Ulysses* (1922). He saw the book as acknowledging the breakdown of 19th-century norms for reporting on life—and, therefore, also rejecting the social assumptions governing novel-writing itself. After 1918, Eliot believed, those assumptions had lost their bearing. In his view, Joyce had had to turn to Homeric myth as a way "of controlling, of ordering, of giving a shape and a significance to the immense panorama of futility and anarchy which is contemporary history." Many years later, one of Faulkner's own novels, *A Fable* [1954], would center on a failed attempt to end World War I early. By mutual consent, Allies and Germans would just refuse to continue fighting. Their effort was doomed; court-martial and execution were the inevitable outcomes. But *A Fable* lets us see that, for Faulkner no less than for his contemporaries, the war was unforgettable not least because it remained unjustifiable.

William Faulkner, 1954, Library of Congress, Prints and Photographs Division, Van Vechten Collection

1

Introduction

A s I have argued, WWI was a major event affecting an entire generation of modernist writers whose careers were launched or already flourishing in the 1920s. Like Faulkner, they refused to write according to familiar 19th-century conventions of plot and character development. Although he did not fight in it, the Great War would haunt Faulkner for decades.

But there was also another war that influenced Faulkner as much as WWI, albeit indirectly. The Civil War had ended 32 years before his birth, but his native South still suffered widespread devastation—physically, politically, and socially. Its values and aspirations had not survived the ravage and humiliation wrought by Ulysses S. Grant and William T. Sherman. Those values and aspirations did not simply disappear, however. Rather, they lingered as reminders of how things used to be—or better, how (decades later) it *seemed* that they used to be. Growing up in Oxford, MS, young Faulkner absorbed stories and myths about the fallen glory of the Confederacy and nostalgia for the Old South.

Even decades after the war ended and the New South emerged with its commitment to commerce and industry, profit and progress, his region remained awash in sentimental war narratives of the Lost Cause. Early on, Faulkner grasped the hollowness of these narratives, even as he found the New South vulgar and repellant. This conflicted situation left him stymied: a useless past saturated in nostalgic fictions and an equally useless future dedicated to soulless materialism. Although the young Faulkner was determined to become a writer, his birthplace bequeathed him less a coherent story to tell than a cluster of shard-like, contradictory realities. When he finally worked this out—after several false starts—the results were not simple.

What added to the complexity of the situation was that people, he realized, did not move through time at the same pace. They did not have the same memories and assumptions and were not headed toward the same goals. If you were a child in such a family, you were immersed in past histories whose repercussions you had no way of understanding. You did not even know about these concealed histories until later—too late to take them into account. And if you were a white child in the American South at the turn of the 20th century, you were (willy-nilly) part of a racial drama that shaped your identity before you ever thought about race. You would have "known" black people long before you encountered them. On this model, real life situations were like icebergs. Most of what actually mattered—what could wreck you if approached without sufficient care—was at first (and often for a long time) out of sight.

Social arrangements of this New South bristled with long-simmering hostilities. But your childhood innocence, however immersed in these arrangements, was incapable of taking their measure. Most starkly, you were born in the midst of interracial dramas that ranged from intimacy to murderous violence. Faulkner absorbed this unstable mix—he was an integral part of it, yet did not see himself as such. He belonged to a family whose ancestors had years earlier done memorable and vicious things. They unleashed a chain of events that spanned and impacted several generations: the grandfathers emotionally wounded their sons who, in turn, inflicted the same pain on their own sons. Young Faulkner, moreover, had been nurtured and embraced by a Negro substitute-mother, Mammy Callie Barr. His culture would teach him, relentlessly, to recognize her as black and different. Yet, he also knew (in body and mind) that she was warm and the same. The fabric of his daily life was soaked in the scandal of ancient wounds and abiding contradictions. It was filled with acknowledgments that enabled and with disownings that crippled. Above all, it was premised on racial convictions and practices that turned a people no different from him into a people utterly different from him.

Faulkner would reach his 30s and write his first two novels before he started to see this clearly—clearly enough to recognize that these social structures and arrangements provided *usable* material for his fiction.

He realized there was a cauldron of race and class tensions percolating beneath the surface of conventions meant to pacify them. Pushing further, approaching the iceberg of Southern realities more closely, he would discover even deeper fissures. His first masterpiece, *The Sound and the Fury* (1929), reveals the Southern family engaged in its own miniature version of Civil War. Although Faulkner began his career as a poet, with this novel he ceased to define himself as poet. He had found that the prose domain of normal life could give him all he would ever need. If penetrated deeply enough, it contained the lyricism, heartbreak, and scandal that he had earlier sought to express through poetry alone. This is how he would create his Yoknapatawpha County (his "little postage stamp of native soil," as he would call it later in *The Paris Review*). There, he would find that the actual and the apocryphal—the prosaic/normal and the poetic/extraordinary—were one and the same.

The tick-tock of clock-time is progressive and ongoing, but if you look harder, you come to a more disturbing model of temporality. Faulkner saw that lives, which were apparently moving forward, might be invisibly arrested or deformed by events from the past because Southerners remained passionately attached to values that had ceased to be viable since 1865—when the South lost the Civil War. All around, a racial divide was hysterically insisted upon yet physiologically groundless. The two races scandalously shared each other's blood. Yet, one had gone to war—and would continue to erupt into violence—in order to keep the other subordinate and its bloodline separate. Shock—what Faulkner calls "outrage"—would become the bass note of his novelistic canvas. *The Sound and the Fury* (like his subsequent masterworks) would center on shock. But this shock had little to do with the trenches or the bombs of World War I. Such war wounds—the central premise of his first novel, *Soldiers' Pay* (1926)—had all along been an exotic alibi. The real shock, the one that tore his protagonists apart, was home-grown. And there was simply no simple way to say that.

It is time now to open up the history of that "little postage stamp of native soil" that Faulkner would recreate as Yoknapatawpha County. In *Absalom, Absalom!* (1936), Faulkner's Southern protagonist, Quentin Compson, tries hard to explain the South to his incredulous Canadian roommate at Harvard. Frustrated, he says: "You can't understand it. You would have to be born there." The South Faulkner was born into struck Quentin—as it struck his author—as both all-explaining and inexplicable to others. The history of actual Oxford and Lafayette County undergirds the doings in his fictional Jefferson and Yoknapatawpha County. Take away the former, and the latter lose their ground and resonance. The place precedes the writer, spurring him—often by its very recalcitrance—to his most remarkable fictional moves.

Lafayette County, in North Central Mississippi, was founded by repeated acts of violence. In taking over this territory in the early 19th century, white settlers had to dislodge the native Chickasaw Indians who had long been living there. (They were forcibly expelled to the "Indian Territory," which later became Oklahoma.) The US government acknowledged Lafayette County's legal status in 1836. Soon enough, in order to produce its major crop, cotton, the region required a cheap and exploitable workforce. That is why it began to import slaves—to labor in the cotton fields. Cotton brought wealth to its planters, the state prospered, and in 1848 Mississippi founded its University in Oxford. The racial politics of town and county were the same. The planters treated those requisite black slaves less as kindred human beings than as animals requiring white surveillance and care. Mississippi hewed tightly to this racial stance—both economically and ideologically. When the Civil War broke out in 1861, the state took only a few weeks longer than South Carolina to determine, defiantly, that it too would secede.

A war, at first distant, soon came home. Grant and Sherman were bent on capturing a Confederate river fortress in Vicksburg and, as they advanced, they laid waste. An earlier strategy of persuasion and reconciliation had hardened into one of punishment: these Southerners had to be brought to heel. Grant took Oxford in December of 1862, and 20 months later the city was burned down. In the aftermath, an imperishable narrative of Yankee wrongdoing was launched, one which young Faulkner grew up with some 40 years later. Although the North won the War in 1865, the South insidiously won it back during the 1870s. It turned out that the promise of Reconstruction—the project of giving former slaves a full American citizenship—was beyond fulfilling. It required more courage, funding, and protection than any post-1865 federal government was willing to provide. By 1875, noting with horror his state's successful denial of civil rights to its black population, Mississippi's Republican Governor Adelbert Ames recognized the heartbreaking irony (as cited by Eric Foner in *Reconstruction*): "A revolution has taken place—by force of arms—and a race are disenfranchised—they are to be returned to a condition of serfdom—an era of second slavery."

Throughout the first half of the 20th century, Mississippi's racial politics strenuously enforced its abusive treatment of blacks. Redneck politicians like Theodore Bilbo and James Vardaman worked to keep it that way. "Six thousand years ago," Vardaman declared in 1903, "the Negro was the same in his native jungle as he is today." A year later, Vardaman, now the Governor, warmed to his topic: "You can scarcely pick up a newspaper whose pages are not blackened with the account of an unmentionable crime committed by a negro brute, and this crime . . . is but the manifestation of the negro's aspiration for social equality." Such was the closed and discriminatory society of the South, with its white and black spaces militantly separated. In 1962, a reluctant President John F. Kennedy would need the National Guard to force segregationist Governor Ross Barnett to allow black military veteran James Meredith to enter the University of Mississippi Law School.

This was the world that young William Faulkner grew up in. How did it affect him? Like all children, he listened to his elders' nostalgic narratives. Indeed, the Civil War was presented to him in sugar-coated terms as the Lost Cause—the New South's conviction that the Old South had been noble and heroic. Over time, he might have sorted out a deeper picture of his region and his family's past. He would probably have noted, early on, his father's surly unease around his own more colorful father. But when would he have begun to recognize a pattern repeating his grandfather's relationship with his own father, the flamboyant Colonel W. C. (William Clark) Falkner? An orphan making his way in 1839 to Pontotoc, MS, the young Falkner had at first been accepted by his maternal aunt and her husband, John Wesley Thompson. But later—and inexplicably—Thompson rejected young Falkner from his burgeoning law practice. Years later, this same Falkner married, fathered a child, and lost his wife. He gave up his baby to the Thompsons, agreeing never to get the boy back. Instead, he remarried and began a second family. The child—J. W. T. (John Wesley Thompson) Falkner—grew up in his adoptive family, becoming in time a successful banker and railway tycoon. But J. W. T. (aka "the Young Colonel") never matched the larger-than-life figure of his biological father, the Old Colonel. He almost certainly knew that he did not. Many years later, at the turn of the 20th century, J. W. T. chose to sell (at a loss) his profitable railroad. He did this at precisely the moment when *his* eldest son Murry was running it efficiently. Subsequently, at the sound of a train whistle, Murry—William's surly father—stopped whatever he was doing and just stared vacantly into space. When would William have decoded his father's wistful stare? When did he grasp something that his great fiction rarely forgets: that wounded fathers find intricate ways to destroy their own sons?

There was perhaps even more to discover in the life story of the fabled Old Colonel. It is possible (according to historian Joel Williamson's painstaking research) that the Old Colonel may have fathered a child with a mulatto slave named Emeline, who lived in his yard in the 1860s. Two decades later, the elderly Old Colonel might have had sexual relations with a much younger mulatto woman named Lena. This Lena might well have been Emeline's daughter. No one doubts that in 1889 the Old Colonel met his end, shot by his enraged business partner, Richard Thurmond. That murder clearly arose out of political competition and humiliation. (The Old Colonel had just defeated Thurmond in a local election and apparently had gone to his house to taunt him.) Was the murder also charged with racial and sexual tensions? After all, Emeline and another of her daughters were mulatto members of Thurmond's family in the 1880s. The Old

Colonel's abuse of Lena—if abuse there was—might have rankled Thurmond no less than the political motives undoubtedly at play. All of this is inevitably speculative. Yet, in 1942, Faulkner wrote *Go Down, Moses*, perhaps his most powerful narrative of paternal abuse. Circuitously, by way of a grandson's later recognitions, it told the story of a white master impregnating his own black slave. Twenty-five years later, that same master, widowed and old, would impregnate that slave's (and his own) daughter. Faulkner was surely seeking to articulate the scandalous substructure of miscegenation that haunted Southern culture. Was he at the same time airing his own family's dirty laundry?

Finally, the Old Colonel takes us, indirectly, to the "u" in Faulkner's name. William's spelling of the name as Faulkner—rather than his family's traditional spelling of Falkner—conveys his bid for fame. He first signed himself as "Faulkner" in 1918, when seeking to get accepted into the Royal Air Force in Toronto. He would later use that spelling, more pointedly, when signing his volume of poems, *The Marble Faun*. There, he identified himself as the "great-grandson of Col. W. C. Faulkner, C.S.A." When asked about the "u" in the Colonel's name, he liked to claim that his ancestor had originally spelled his name with a "u," but he had changed it to Falkner after discovering some "no-good" folks living nearby named Faulkner. With this account, the great-grandson was merely restoring an earlier reality. However, there was more at stake—a child's bid for independence and his own identity. He was, as William Faulkner, erasing two generations of Falkners who stood between him and his famous ancestor. We will never know the precise motive, but my use of both "Faulkner" and "Falkner" in this book refers to an intricate family history. It does not indicate a lazy job of proofreading.

At the beginning of his life, William Faulkner, the future novelist, was known as Billy Falkner. He never wrote directly about his early years, and he abhorred confession of every sort. Given the dearth of information, we can only speculate about the inner dimensions of his childhood. The first of four sons (born in New Albany, MS on July 5, 1897), he was a querulous, colicky infant. His mother Maud had to rock him for hours each night in order to soothe him into sleep;

coincidentally or not, he would be a light, easily troubled sleeper his whole life. Family moves (to Ripley in 1898 and then to Oxford in 1902) forced young Billy to reconfigure his sense of his surroundings. And his privileged status as an only child was soon shattered by the births of his three brothers. The last one, Dean, came into the world in 1907 and required sustained attention from Maud. She had just lost her own mother; between her grief over that loss and Dean's infantile needs, not much of her heart may have been left over for 10-year-old Billy.

Maud Butler Falkner's impress on her son is difficult to summarize. We know that, throughout his life, he composed his fiction on a spindle-legged desk she had given him, while seated in a tall-backed chair that was also a gift from his mother. These facts speak powerfully to her hold on Faulkner's imagination. Unlike her outdoorsy, unlettered husband, Murry, Maud was also a practitioner of the arts. She painted during much of her life, and she was an avid proponent of literature. She introduced her oldest son to the Bible, as well as to the writings of William Shakespeare, Miguel de Cervantes, and the 19th-century novelists. Later on, she defended his fiction, however iconoclastic. Murry—who seems never to have read any novel his son wrote—once complained to his wife about the scandal that *Sanctuary*, the 1931 novel about the rape of a young co-ed, provoked in Oxford. Maud replied, "Let him alone, Buddy, he writes what he has to." Maud mattered immeasurably to William, yet we find few positive portraits of her in his fiction. His first masterpiece, *The Sound and the Fury*, goes alarmingly the other way: the character of Mrs. Compson reveals a mother who is uniquely damaging to her offspring. When William was a child and Maud determined that his posture was sloppy, she made him wear an uncomfortable back brace for two years. Can it be accidental that the odious Mrs. Compson forced her daughter Caddy to wear one too?

Father figures fare better in Faulkner's novels, but only slightly. Murry was in fundamental ways his oldest son's opposite: he was tall (like his own father and grandfather) while William was short; he was blunt-featured while William had his mother's finely chiseled brows and lips; and he was unlettered while William was precociously literary. Perhaps most of all, he seems to have been uninterested in the intricacies of the inner life. (His favorite reading was the Sunday comic strips in the newspapers.) Murry's relations with his eldest son were strained and uncomprehending. When he tried once to improve their relationship, matters only got worse. Faulkner loved to repeat the anecdote about his father finding out that William had taken up smoking. To Murry, this discovery provided an opportunity to bond with his oldest child. One night, he took out a cigar and offered his son a "good smoke." William accepted and reached into his pocket for his pipe. He then broke the cigar in half, stuffed one-half into his pipe, and lit it. Watching this, Murry said nothing, then left the room. "He never gave me another cigar," Faulkner gleefully recalled.

Faulkner would undoubtedly learn most about bad marriages from his own troubled union with Estelle Oldham, but that of his parents gave him some early glimpses into incompatibility between spouses. Maud apparently sought from Murry a culture-enriched responsiveness that he could not provide. He, on the other hand, needed a bodily tenderness toward his shortcomings that she could not proffer. Unfocused after his father sold the railroad, Murry found a self-destructive way to take his revenge. He gave up on his career and began to drink with greater abandon, following an old Falkner "tradition"—traceable back to the Old Colonel and operative in each generation of males thereafter—of excessive drinking. Maud sought to turn Murry's periodic "drying out" cures into a pedagogic demonstration. She insisted that her sons join them on the ritual trek to Keeley's Institute, 15 miles from Memphis, to witness their father's ongoing humiliation.

Although Murry would become Business Manager of the University of Mississippi in his later years, the job required little labor. What labor it did require involved a kind of work he did not enjoy. A taciturn outdoorsman, he loved stables, carriages, and horses far more than doing bookkeeping for a university. Probably, even more, he loved trains—until his father sold his railroad out from under him. Murry's drinking eventually led to health problems, including a heart condition, and he died of a heart attack in 1932—almost exactly 30 years before William too succumbed to the same condition. Working in Hollywood at the time of Murry's death, William did not find it necessary to attend the funeral. In retrospect, we can see that Murry had been overmastered by a stronger-willed spouse. He had also been eclipsed by a famous son who ignored him. As though to erase his identity even further, the local obituary spelled his name as "Faulkner." Years later, as Maud was nearing her own death, she asked William about the afterlife. "Will I have to see your father there?" she wondered. "No," Faulkner answered, "not if you don't want to." "That's good," she said, "I never did like him." That Faulkner enjoyed this vignette as much as the cigar one gives us the mean-spirited measure of his relations with his father.

What might it have been like for a sensitive oldest son to grow up in this household? Again, we can only speculate since Faulkner himself never talked about such matters. Some insight, however, can be gleaned from his brothers, who write in their later memoirs of a happy childhood full of shared, Twain-like misadventures. But what emerges with equal force from their accounts is William's unapproachability. He grew up in their midst, remained loyal and supportive, and impressed them indelibly. Yet, they did not know him well. For him, childhood may not have been Twain-like at all. He had once written his great aunt that her niece, the "quick and dark" Natalie, "must have carried me." In the same letter, he spoke of her as "touching me" during "one of those spells of loneliness and nameless sorrow that children suffer." He was perhaps sensitized to touch as only a child who has not been touched enough may be. His own mother was obviously there for him throughout his life—a model of rectitude and fidelity that he always honored. Yet, at a deeper bodily level, she may not have been there at all. It was probably Mammy Callie, not Maud Falkner, who attended most intimately to Billy's childrearing. They all lived in the same house, but each in his or her own way—spatially together, yet speechlessly apart.

We may speculate that childhood wrought upon William the experience of being little among others who were big. No less, it might have given him something his own fiction renders unforgettably: the experience of not knowing, of coming to the family history not at its beginning but in the middle. He was discovering that others acted out of motives he would come to recognize only later—or not at all. Their impact on him was nonetheless unavoidable; in fact, he might have grasped, childhood was about unavoidability. It was about being in a body not yet able to avoid encounters it had not chosen to have. Some of childhood's sorrows—as he had mentioned to his great-aunt—would remain forever inexplicable. But other sorrows might open up to understanding—later—when things did open up. And he perhaps recognized that, without having chosen it, his own childhood had launched him toward a personal silence, an inwardness beyond relinquishing. Strangest of all, this took place in the presence of others sharing his household space.

To tell this in its intricacy would require something more than Mark Twain's narrative resources. He would need to show how what is shared is doubled by what is unsharable. No less, he would need to show how what namelessly assaults the child now had namable roots in what had happened before he was born but could be discovered—if at all—only later. Childhood, he seemed to grasp, was about double exposure: the sudden violence of *is*, juxtaposed against the clarifying context of *was*. In 1957, he would tell this to a class of students at the University of Virginia: "Maybe peace is only a condition in retrospect, when the subconscious has got rid of the gnats and the tacks and the broken glass in experience and has left only the peaceful pleasant things—that was peace. Maybe peace is not is, but was." The later retrospect of *was* looks back, frames, and clarifies the immediacy of *is*. Childhood's significance opens up later, even as it is actually lived in the present. Could he ever get words to say *that*?

There was, at least, one person in Oxford who might have thought he could. Phil Stone was a Yale graduate, a University of Oxford alumnus, and the intellectual scion of a local aristocratic planter family. Several years older than Faulkner, he was on the lookout for promising young Mississippians. Was Stone seeking to escape his own loneliness by sharing his gifted sensibility with that of another Southerner? Was he looking for a mirror in which he might recognize his own unexpressed possibilities? Whatever his motives, he took young Faulkner under his wing. He gave him poetry and fiction to read, and he appointed himself (unasked) as the young man's mentor.

For the decade between 1915 and 1925 Stone would serve as Faulkner's stimulus, critic, friend, book-lender, and would-be war comrade. He would also serve as the patron who funded (in 1924) the publication of Faulkner's first book of poems, *The Marble Faun.*

Unquestionably, the young Faulkner imagined his future as that of a poet. He not only wrote verse from his teens forward, but that verse aggressively called attention to its identity *as verse*: by jettisoning all (local) prosaic surroundings. It teemed with fauns and satyrs, battened on classical narratives, was intent on fashioning a world elsewhere. The late 19th-century British poet, Algernon Charles Swinburne, appealed precisely to Faulkner's longings for escape: "At the age of sixteen, I discovered Swinburne," Faulkner wrote in 1924. "Or rather Swinburne discovered me, springing from some tortured undergrowth of my adolescence, like a highwayman, making me his slave." On at least two fronts Swinburne would have been hard to resist. His verse, heavily rhymed and rhythmical, labored to transport its reader to exotic settings—to not-Mississippi. Swinburne's settings were drenched in pagan references; they were defiantly anti-Christian. As he wrote in his *Hymn to Proserpina*, "Thou hast conquered, O pale Galilean, the world has grown gray from thy breath." Swinburne rejected the deathliness of the dispensation that Christ (the "pale Galilean") brought into the world. His poetry signaled a passionate bid for bodily liberation from Christian prohibitions—the liberation that was strictly forbidden by the Presbyterian norms blanketing the Oxford Faulkner grew up in.

This liberal orientation toward the body would remain in Faulkner's life and work. In *Light in August*, nine years later, a central female character named Lena will embody something of Swinburne's appeal. Impregnated by one man, Lena chooses to make her way unhurriedly through the countryside, walking on foot from Alabama to Mississippi. She remains casually receptive to the prospect of finding in her travels a better man than the one who got her pregnant and then ditched her. She is not bothered by the issue of legitimacy. Lena—her name alluding (Faulkner later acknowledged) to the Greek Helen of Troy—stands out luminously in *Light in August*. Faulkner powerfully juxtaposes her bodily plenitude against the (male) crucifixions and self-crucifixions erupting all around her. But this was to come later.

Reading Faulkner's poetry in 1915 or 1916, Phil Stone was sufficiently moved by their passion to underwrite their publication. More, he would continue to claim—long past the time when the claim made sense—that Faulkner missed his true vocation when he became a novelist. *The Marble Faun*, for its part, would enter the literary world without making the slightest splash.

Stone plays a significant role in Faulkner's career. But the central figure in his emotional development was a lively young woman about his age, Estelle Oldham. She was the daughter of a prominent Oxford family that lived not far from the Falkners. The two were mere teenagers when they first met. Over time, they began to see each other with increasing frequency. Voluble and charming (as he would never be), Estelle sustained an intricate inner life as well. She loved to read—enough to be delighted with this silent boy already carrying inside himself a teeming world of thoughts and feelings. Estelle captivated most of the young men in Oxford and was the most popular figure at the dances. Yet, she set her sights on Faulkner, eventually getting him to share more and more of his poetry and aspirations. By the time they were nearing 20, they were deeply (but unofficially) bound to each other. They knew they would marry—when the right moment came.

That moment did not come. In its place came a bid for Estelle's hand from one Cornell Franklin. He was the handsome son of an eminent Mississippi family, who graduated from the University of Mississippi with all the honors it could bestow. Clearly destined for a successful legal career, he was hard to turn down. Nor did Estelle—quite—turn him down. Franklin may not even have known about his rival, Faulkner, who in 1918—the critical year in their relationship—hardly looked like a good bet. Known already for immoderate drinking, recognized as maybe talented but certainly moody and difficult, he seemed no match for Franklin. Sure of his acceptance, Franklin sent Estelle an expensive engagement ring from Honolulu (where he held a prestigious job at the port). The two families began to elaborate plans for a big April wedding. As though paralyzed by the force of this new development (a consequence of her belle-of-the-ball charm), Estelle became desperate. She pressed

Faulkner for a last-minute elopement; she would flee if he would. There was still time. For reasons we will never know but which must have caused him anguish for years to come, he refused to elope, insisting that they get their parents' consent. He must have realized that this would fail; both sets of parents immediately opposed their union. So Estelle married Cornell Franklin in April 1918, and Faulkner fled with Phil Stone to New Haven, CT. Ostensibly he wanted to fight in the Great War. More urgently, he had to escape from unbearable emotional distress.

Here the scene changes from tragic to comic. In New Haven, Stone and Faulkner set about inventing zany ways of getting into a war that was nearing its end. Faulkner had earlier been turned down from the air division of the US Army because he was too short, by half an inch, and too light, by a few pounds. But the British Royal Air Force, operating out of Toronto, did not follow these protocols. So, pretending to be British (not the first and not the last of Faulkner's masquerades), they managed to get into a Royal Air Force training program. Stone soon dropped out, but not Faulkner. For months he trained in Toronto, writing his parents about his fascination with the military and the innards of airplanes. (His pencil drawings of the planes, accompanying some of the letters, are exquisitely detailed.) The War ended in November of 1918, and a month later Faulkner returned home to Oxford. He arrived at the train station regally decked out in an officer's uniform he had bought from a veteran but was not entitled to wear. He was also carrying a cane to help him cope with a war-wound in the knee—supposedly incurred while flying over France in the last dark days of the war. This wound was invented out of whole cloth. It serves as a metaphor for Faulkner's larger narrative of a turbulent war experience for which no evidence exists. He got his wings only in late December, over a month after Armistice. The self-proclaimed aviator who had been shot down over France hardly knew how to fly a plane.

The comedy of masquerades continued. Pretending to be a wounded veteran, Faulkner was admitted as a special student at the University of Mississippi. (He would have needed this veteran-status. Having deliberately refused to go past the 11th grade, he was not otherwise a candidate for college). His university classmates were not slow in noting and mocking his airs. "Count No-Count," they called this attitudinizing figure who postured as a war-wounded veteran familiar with the latest French poetry. After a year or so, this pretense of jaded sophistication was wearing thin, and Faulkner was becoming increasingly restless. He left the university and returned to the Northeast, where he worked for Lord and Taylor's in New York for the better part of a year. Bored with that job and uncertain what to do next, he then embarked on probably the most preposterous masquerade of his life: he accepted, not without misgivings, the position of Postmaster of the University of Mississippi. The ever-enterprising Phil Stone had pulled political strings to get the position offered to Faulkner. Although it was virtually a sinecure—the postal area he oversaw was tiny—Faulkner royally mishandled it. He just could not get himself to take other people's mail seriously. (He was, however, not above rifling through their magazines and "borrowing" the ones he found interesting.) After three years of such cavalier behavior and the complaints that steadily accrued, the Post Office fired him. Walking away from the job, he got off a final riposte: "I reckon I'll be at the beck and call of folks with money all my life, but thank God I won't ever again have to be at the beck and call of every son of a bitch who's got two cents to buy a stamp."

Soon he was on to the next masquerade: several months spent in New Orleans, in early 1925. Thanks to the Lord and Taylor job, he had met Elizabeth Prall in New York. Subsequently, she had married the novelist Sherwood Anderson. They were living a bohemian life in New Orleans, and she invited Faulkner to visit them. In an atypical move, he accepted her offer. His visit was to be but a stopgap; the real voyage he had in mind (in this, echoing Ezra Pound and T. S. Eliot before him) was to Europe. En route, he traveled to New Orleans, where he met the group of avant-garde writers gathered around Anderson. Thanks to the tremendous success of *Winesburg, Ohio* (1919), Anderson had become famous. Making the most of his celebrity, he had attracted a virtual colony of practicing and would-be writers and artists. From all reports, they were having one hell of a good time. The siren call of New Orleans would have been hard for this Northern Mississippian to resist. He had spent years persevering in heavy drinking despite the local strictures against it. His iconoclastic bent had more than once got him into trouble in hide-bound Oxford. In New Orleans, however, he found—and would celebrate for decades—a welcome emancipation from the Presbyterian pieties he had long chafed under. Indeed, New Orleans seemed to serve as a setting for a perpetual holiday. The Anderson gang caroused all day and drank all night—all the while talking, talking, talking... Faulkner had come to New Orleans for a few weeks, but he stayed for a few months.

Finally, though, the unsentimental critic lodged deep inside Faulkner's imagination had had enough. It was time to quit the talk-engorged antics of the Anderson Circle and book his passage for Europe. Before his disenchantment set in, however, a foundational change of vocation had occurred. Anderson and his coterie had persuaded the restless young Faulkner—less on purpose than gradually and by multiple examples—to change his calling. He would no longer be a poet, but instead, become a novelist. He would go to Paris later that fall where—refocused and energized—he would complete his first novel begun in New Orleans, *Soldiers' Pay*.

2

Stumbling into Fame

The 1930s are widely recognized as Faulkner's most creative decade. *The Sound and the Fury* (1929) opened the floodgates, permitting his subsequent novels, *As I Lay Dying* (1930), *Sanctuary* (1931), and *Light in August* (1932) to emerge in flawless lockstep. A brief hiatus occurred in the early 1930s: his "biggest" masterpiece, *Absalom, Absalom!* required more brooding and revising than he anticipated. But once it was released in 1936, *The Unvanquished* (1938), and *The Hamlet* (1940) followed swiftly, rounding out a peerless decade of productivity. Throughout this decade, Faulkner was the "hottest" novelist in America.

Looking back, we can see that crises he encountered during the five preceding years made that later flowering possible. These were the years in which, stumbling, he came into his own. He also seemed to recognize that *stumbling* was his most powerful subject. Whether he called it "outrage" or "assault," the core insight was the same: when life "abrupts" (his verb from *Absalom, Absalom!*) upon us, we stumble and are out of control. By 1930, after the publication of *The Sound and the Fury* and *As I Lay Dying*, he had made this insight his own, becoming the genius we know as Faulkner. What disorienting experiences during those five years "prepared" him for such a bout of productivity?

In 1925, he was still in the mode of what I referred to in the previous chapter as "masquerade"—pretending to be someone he was not. He traveled to Europe, likely envisaging that these four months abroad would follow the scenario made famous by the careers of Pound and Eliot: of Europe being the "mother culture." On this model,

Europe (including England) supplied culturally enriched experiences and inspiration to budding American writers. In those days, London and Paris were "sacred" destinations for expatriate artists. Such pilgrimages saw their heyday during the flowering of modernist art occurring in Paris before and after the Great War.

Yet France (a country Faulkner adored, and one that adored him back) would never offer him fertile territory. His most ambitiously troubled novel, *A Fable* (1954), takes place on its shores during WWI. Despite endless revising, *A Fable* never takes off into the air—probably because it never roots itself deeply enough into its foreign soil. In 1925, when Faulkner set for Europe, he did not know that, like the Greek god Antaeus, he was powerful only when on native soil. Even though Sherwood Anderson had given him an introduction to James Joyce, then living in Paris, Faulkner was too shy to approach the celebrated author of *Ulysses*. He may have dreamed of a "European career," but he never pursued that dream aggressively. Indeed, his shyness towards Joyce foreshadowed a lifelong withdrawal from the ceremonial trappings of literary fame. He would later turn down the overtures of younger writers seeking him out just as, in 1925, he was unwilling to make such overtures toward Joyce. Perhaps because of this innate reticence, he described himself in the late 1930s, at the end of his most prolific decade, as a farmer, not a writer.

Another reason that Faulkner did not adapt well to European surroundings was that his New Orleans experience with Anderson and his crew had fostered in him a new sense of vocation. Pound and Eliot were broadly Western *poets*, but he came away from New Orleans determined to become a specifically American *novelist*. He had written, while there, several prose pieces for a local newspaper. More tellingly, he was finishing a novel centered on American materials.

In *Soldiers' Pay*, however, another kind of masquerade holds sway. That novel centers on the betrayals befalling a wounded soldier of the Great War. As such, it cannot but further the masquerade of Faulkner's own war experience. Indeed, it functions as a bid to get that masquerade accepted as truth. (Others did accept it as true. Not until a decade after Faulkner's death in 1962 did it become widely known that he had not seen action in 1918.) By contrast, Dos Passos, E.E.

Cummings, and Hemingway had actually been there. All three had suffered in the war; Hemingway had been grievously wounded. Their books, *Three Soldiers*, *The Enormous Room*, and *A Farewell to Arms* respectively, draw on their authors' personal experiences. We might ask: how can *Soldiers' Pay* compel its reader, even though the war experience it seems founded on was never Faulkner's own?

One of Faulkner's best commentators, André Bleikasten, urged readers to think of the writer's prevarications as something more than lies—as "corrective" fictions, attempts to make reality align with his subjective sense of what was supposed to have happened—but didn't. From this perspective, *Soldiers' Pay* becomes luminous. The fatal wound it testifies to on every page is imaginatively real. No reader of that novel has trouble believing that the protagonist, Donald Mahan, is dying—and that he is being betrayed, post-war, by many people he had earlier trusted. If it fails to be one of Faulkner's greater novels, it is because he was just learning the craft of fiction. The novel is full of vivid shards—memorable scenes of deracinated veterans now stranded at home; it shows as well an incipient grasp of what may be seen as musical structure. Contrapuntally, the novel shifts from setting to setting, character to character, vignette to vignette. But the settings, characters, and vignettes tend to remain confined to their local space. What is missing is the *glue*—the narrative necessity that would solder these parts indissolubly, forging a design to which each part indirectly contributes. This structural problem—what we might consider as a whole that is less than the sum of its parts—will beset Faulkner's second novel (*Mosquitoes*, 1927) as well. He will overcome it in *Flags in the Dust* (his third novel), and he will transcend it in the fourth one, *The Sound and the Fury* (1929).

Before 1929, however, Faulkner did not seem to recognize his major challenges as a writer. He needed to learn not just how to get the pieces of his novels to relate more compellingly to each other but, even more crucially, he had to learn how to suppress his delegated narrator and get him out of the fictional performance. The narrative voice that tells the first three novels makes them possible, but it also makes them second-rate: that "smart" Southern voice keeps drawing attention to itself. Once Faulkner managed to make it disappear, his materials suddenly came alive, speaking hypnotically for themselves and enacting their different ways of *stumbling*. With these changes, his work began to jell. Indeed, these novels' separate materials became so intensely bonded as to release an incandescent force-field of thought and feeling. A reader of his fiction written between 1929 and 1931—*The Sound and the Fury, As I Lay Dying,* and *Sanctuary*—comes away wondering how work of such conceptual intricacy can also hit home emotionally, like a sledge-hammer.

All this would begin to occur by 1929, but we cannot leave Faulkner's European adventure of late 1925 without elaborating further on the stakes of his decision to return home when he did. The trip served as Faulkner's single temptation to follow a Pound/Eliot model of Euro-creativity, which aspired toward forms of alienation and citation-insistent worldliness not available on American shores. One thinks of Eliot's *The Waste Land* (1922) and its incessant parade of snippets from earlier cultures, each of them signaling the writer's ultra-sophisticated world-weariness. For well over a decade, this poem bestrode the Anglo-American cultural scene as *the* text to emulate. Though Faulkner would draw on Eliot's poem, he would (more resonantly) resist its siren-like appeal. No reader of his great fiction has the sense of entering the high-art sanctuary of Eliot's celebrated poem. Somehow Faulkner grasped that European cultural materials—the allure of an older world of finer values—were for him less a beacon than a dead end. After four months abroad he had to go home—and not just because he was out of money. Home was that "little postage stamp of native soil" that was waiting for him on the other side of the Atlantic.

I mentioned some of the defects of *Soldiers' Pay*. Faulkner's next novel, *Mosquitoes* (1927), also suffered from several shortcomings. It too could be considered a masquerade, in the sense that its narrator engages its materials with implicit mockery and unremitting detachment. *Mosquitoes* focuses on New Orleans antics Faulkner had witnessed and participated in. Seen later from an estranging distance, such foolish behavior tends to reduce to the juvenile silliness of adults who have not grown up. The narration of their doings exposes each of them with unforgiving precision. No reader is likely to relate to this cast of characters—thinly disguised versions of the New Orleans gang

Faulkner had known in 1925. This is because Faulkner's narrator doesn't care for them either. More damagingly, the narrator attempts a sophisticated, Aldous Huxley-type of knowing humor. This is a tone Faulkner cannot make attractive. (Faulkner's humor when it works, is savage and disturbing. But he needs a Jason Compson from *The Sound and the Fury* or a Joe Brown from *Light in August* to make it work.) Despite such flaws, *Mosquitoes* got a green light from Horace Liveright—New York's premier publisher of American modernist literature. Liveright had been captivated, the year before, by *Soldiers' Pay*'s musical rhythms and its elegant despair. He brought that novel out in 1926 and signed on to publish *Mosquitoes* in 1927. He was determined not to lose this young genius.

Within a year, however, Liveright had had enough of Faulkner. Faced with the manuscript of his third novel, *Flags in the Dust*, Liveright's judgment was unconditional: he flatly turned the book down, imploring Faulkner not to show it to any other publisher. He doubtless meant well, but his words stung Faulkner to the core: "*Soldiers' Pay* was a very fine book and should have done better. . . *Mosquitoes* wasn't quite so good . . . Now comes *Flags in the Dust* and we're frankly very much disappointed." Faulkner read Liveright's assessment as a pitiless summary of his career to date. Thirty years old, he was the author of a volume of poetry no one wanted to buy and of two novels few readers paid much attention to. Now he saw himself rejected by one of the most powerful publishers in America. Desperately, he tried to salvage *Flags*, eventually leaving the revisions to his friend Ben Wasson. It was too depressing for him to continue on his own.

Flags was not the worst of his troubles in 1928. Estelle Oldham Franklin—whom he had failed to elope with, whom he was unable to forget—had come back into his life. Divorced from her husband after several years of a marriage gone irreparably sour, and now a mother of two small children, she returned to Oxford in the mid-1920s. She turned toward Faulkner as a lifeline. Their courtship resumed, as passionate as before but more troubled than ever. At 20, he had been a markedly taciturn young man, given to excessive drinking. Now, a decade later, Faulkner had become more aggressively anti-social.

Further, with three published books under his belt, he had solidified his mantle of a Bohemian Writer. Estelle must have recognized that it would be hard, maybe impossible, to change him, but her life was a mess, and she needed a husband urgently enough to accept these challenges. He, however, was not so sure he needed a wife. He had been uncertain in 1918 and now, a decade later, whatever had separated them before had grown in density and recalcitrance.

Though pressed by Estelle, he kept putting off a date for the marriage. Soon Estelle's sister, Dot, was working on him to step up to his responsibilities. Finally, he set the date. Then—frantic over what he was about to sign on to—he wrote his friend and publisher, Hal Smith, the following:

> I am going to be married. Both want to and have to. THIS PART IS CONFIDENTIAL, UTTERLY. For my honor and the sanity—I believe life—of a woman. This is not bunk; nor am I being sucked in. We grew up together and I don't think she could fool me in this way; that is, make me believe that her mental condition, her nerves are this far gone. . . . It's a situation which I engendered and permitted to ripen which has become unbearable, and I am tired of running from the devilment I bring about.

At the time, Faulkner was completing his bleakest novel, *Sanctuary*. It cannot be accidental that he set June 20 as the date on which its protagonist, Temple Drake, enters a courthouse and perjures herself. That was the very day he set for contracting a marriage that must have seemed to him as a sort of perjury as well. Temple, in time, would find it impossible to get beyond her all-damaging mistakes. The same may be true for her creator.

Flags in the Dust, which Faulkner completed in 1927, cannot keep the company of the four masterpieces that followed it in the next five years. Yet, Faulkner was not mistaken when he told Liveright (on submitting the manuscript): "At last and certainly, I have written THE book, of which those other things were but foals. I believe it is the damdest best book you'll look at this year, and any other publisher." In hindsight, we can perhaps see better why Liveright was blind to the book's merits. He was a New York publisher intent on upsetting parochial sensibilities—on honoring Pound's modernist dictum, "Make it new." He would have had little trouble recognizing *Soldiers' Pay*'s appeal because it belonged to a burgeoning American genre—the "lost generation" novel—and held its own in that company. In *Mosquitoes*, Liveright would have appreciated Faulkner's superior stance toward a colony of would-be artists and writers. These were sophisticated figures being mocked by an even more knowing narrator, providing grist for Liveright's "smart" New York mill. With *Flags*, however, the discernable genre and the sophisticated tone were absent.

He couldn't see that in *Flags* Faulkner began to make that "postage stamp of native soil" his own, recognizing that his region's history—as broad as Southern heartbreak, as narrow as family legend—was inexhaustibly *writable*. It would take two more novels before Faulkner gave his county its fictional name, Yoknapatawpha (in *As I Lay Dying*). But the county, though unnamed, was born in *Flags*. The book draws centrally on once-aristocratic families, the Sartorises, and the Benbows. It draws as well on a roster of community figures ranging from garrulous old white men to deranged white youths and low-lives, as well as to a hill-country family nestled in the backwoods and steeped in earlier ways. And this is not to mention its three generations of black servants managing to eke out their lives under inattentive white masters. *Flags* is in no hurry to get its story told—something Liveright misread as "you don't seem to have any story to tell." He did not grasp—as many others in 1927 would not have understood—that Faulkner was making his debut as a *Southern* writer. He was showing, with wide-angled, nonjudgmental attention, what happened if you had stayed home during the Great War: you remained enclosed within an enervated, quietly suffocating set of outdated rituals of thinking, feeling, and doing, slowly wasting away. But if you had participated in that war, you found yourself, on return, incapable of communicating to anyone the brutality of your experience. Worse, you were unequipped to make peace with the slow-paced Southern pieties you had departed from.

Flags was Faulkner's first novel about the South, *his* South. That's what it can do. No less instructive is what it cannot do—according to the measure that Faulkner himself would provide two years later in *The Sound and the Fury*. A comparison of two scenes of emotional intensity (one from each novel) brings this point home. We begin with the relatively traditional rhetoric of *Flags*. Here is the protagonist, Bayard Sartoris, wounded and asleep, watched over by Narcissa Benbow, whom he eventually marries. His anguish erupts swiftly:

> He made an indescribable sound, and she turned her head quickly and saw his body straining terrifically in its cast, and his clenched hands and the snarl of his teeth beneath his lifted lip, and as she sat blanched and incapable of further movement he made the sound again. His breath hissed between his teeth and he screamed, a wordless sound that sank into a steady violence of profanity; and when she rose at last and stood over him with her hands against her mouth, his body relaxed and from beneath his sweating brow he watched her with wide intent eyes in which terror lurked, and mad, cold fury, and questioning despair.

Narrated in standard syntax and a hyperbolic vocabulary, this scene invites us to look on from our distance. Its prose reveals, as well, the threadbareness of predictable formulae. Bayard's sound is "indescribable," for Faulkner can describe it only from the perspective of a narrator observing someone else's distress. Faulkner uses Narcissa to provide physical cues for how to read Bayard's torment: his terrific straining, her "blanched" paralysis echoing his "clenched" paralysis, his hissing breath and wordless scream. Like an orgasm, his body relaxes after this release. Yet, Faulkner can articulate what is going on *inside* Bayard only through a roster of familiar nouns like "terror," "fury," and "despair." This could be Joseph Conrad relying on the same well-worn vocabulary to articulate Lord Jim's torment. Both writers understood that their target (the traumatized psyche) was "unspeakable." But neither knows (Conrad never, Faulkner not yet) that it is "unspeakable" only within conventional strategies for narrating the psyche as a coherent entity unified in time and space.

Flags conveys Bayard's distress: he is caught up in a traumatic afterlife of previous events. He is still at that earlier stage, overtaken and penetrated. Something unspeakable happened in the war and holds him prisoner now. The closest Faulkner comes to unlocking Bayard's inner wound is to describe it as ruptured "with ghosts of a thing high-pitched as a hysteria." Faulkner has no interest in narrating this "thing high-pitched;" he focuses instead on its disturbing aftereffects. Bayard attracts Faulkner to the extent that he is "absent" here and now, beyond the reach of therapy. Intensity of portrait and dysfunction of character go hand in hand. Bayard's distress was obviously based on that of Donald Mahan, the wounded protagonist of *Soldiers' Pay*. But Faulkner has not yet figured out how to craft the prose that—in yoking then with now, there with here—will dance its manic fusion inside Bayard and make his wound come to life. He finally figures it out in the tormented Quentin Compson of *The Sound and the Fury*:

> *I have committed incest I said Father it was I it was not Dalton Ames.* And when he put Dalton Ames. Dalton Ames. Dalton Ames. When he put the pistol in my hand I didn't. That's why I didn't. He would be there and she would and I would. Dalton Ames. Dalton Ames. Dalton Ames. If we could have just done something so dreadful and Father said That's sad too people cannot do anything that dreadful they cannot do anything very dreadful at all they cannot even remember tomorrow what seemed dreadful today and I said, You can shirk all things and he said, Ah can you. And I will look down and see my murmuring bones and the deep water like wind, like a roof of wind, and after a long time they cannot distinguish even bones upon the lonely and inviolate sand. Until on the day when He says Rise only the flat-iron would come floating up. It's not when you realise that nothing can help you—religion, pride, anything—it's when you realise that you don't need any aid. Dalton Ames. Dalton Ames. Dalton Ames. If I could have been his mother lying with open body lifted laughing, holding his father with my hand refraining, seeing, watching him die before he lived. *One minute she was standing in the door.*

To find his way into Quentin's ungrammatical anguish, Faulkner had to rupture proper syntax. No less, Quentin's mind is no longer treated as something unified in space and time. Traditional narrative frames its materials in sentences shaped by subject, verb, and predicate. Such decorous sentences render *Flags*'s Bayard as a coherent doer performing his discrete deed (however troubled). But not Quentin. Faulkner's prose for writing him has broken free. Quentin's phrases either lack verbs or mix them up indiscriminately—present perfect, past, conditional, conditional perfect, present, future. The 19th-century tools for representation that Faulkner inherited could only narrate character as a something seen from a distance and gathered into wholeness, in black and white, so to speak. By contrast, Faulkner knew that the psyche under enormous stress was radically different—it was in motion, in full color, penetrated by absent forces, hurtling through space and time.

To articulate that color, Faulkner's prose had to reposition his character's mind in space, time, and the field of others. Most of all, Faulkner had to get his own narrator out of the scene of writing. He had to dramatize his character's distress as though it were happening on its own, without Faulkner's narrator telling it. Thus, we get Quentin's frantic mind careening between different spaces and nonsequential times. No less, this Quentin is drowning in the force-field of absent others. Spaces in this passage lose their distinctiveness. Events that happened in different places are narratively jumbled together—which is exactly how they explode within Quentin's distressed mind. The scene the previous summer with Caddy's first lover, Dalton Ames, shifts abruptly to his dark conversations with Father. Then Faulkner takes us to Quentin's fantasy of looking down on himself as a suicide so deep in the waters of the Charles River that even Christ's call for resurrection will fail to make him stir. Finally, Faulkner takes the reader to Quentin's even stranger fantasy of being secretly present at Ames's conception. In this fantasy, incredibly, Quentin imagines himself as Ames's mother removing Ames's father's penis just before ejaculation, thus killing Ames before he could be conceived.

Faulkner deranges the representation of time even more forcefully. He presses together the Dalton Ames moment, the Caddy at the door moment, and the moment with Father. Pressed together, yet kept apart: the moments are not fused but confused. Time's forward motion (perhaps the deepest assumption our sanity requires and that conventional narrative blessedly supplies) disappears. Finally, the clamorousness of absent others inside the self is beyond pacifying. Quentin's mind is a defective transformer; incompatible human voices pass through it like electric charges. He is a figure composed of screaming phrases, some spoken, some remembered, some fantasized, none assimilated, and none forgettable. In Quentin Compson, Faulkner produced his most memorable character caught in multiple times and splayed out into multiple spaces. No less, Quentin is penetrated by multiple others, most of them absent. It is inconceivable that any of this could be said in a simple fashion.

The sound and fury of distress: the phrasing registers both the title of Faulkner's first masterpiece and its core concern. Or (to use Faulknerian terms introduced earlier), life as it assaults us in the fierce zoom lens of *is*. This is present consciousness under stress, its jagged edges unsoftened by the retrospective wide-angled ordering of *was*. Opening this novel in the disordered mind of the idiot Benjy Compson, Faulkner narrates events before any reader can understand them. He hurls us into the glass before it has been retrospectively cleansed of its gnats, tacks, and fissures. The passage quoted above comes from the second chapter, the monologue of Benjy's suicidal brother, Quentin. The third chapter will attend to the embittered third brother, Jason. Each chapter adheres claustrophobically to the limited optics available to its distressed first-person narrator. Only in the final chapter does Faulkner seek to bring it all together. And it does come together as a Southern tragedy narrated (in three of its four chapters) during Easter weekend in 1928. But no grace hovers on the novel's horizon—there is no risen Christ to save the lost Compsons.

Yet, when the novel ends, we come away with a feeling that is the opposite of *Macbeth*'s nihilistic phrase, "signifying nothing." Instead, we all but choke on how much Faulkner has managed to signify in barely 200 pages. We now know the mother who will not mother, the father who is drinking himself to death, and the blacks who do their best to keep this collapsing family from falling apart faster. Most of all, we know the unparented and disoriented Compson children: the disabled Benjy, the suicidal Quentin, the runaway Caddy (the only girl), and the last boy, Jason. He, it turns out, is the only one still standing in 1928 (the novel's present time). Yet, now grown up, Jason is the most abusive of them all. This entire family history is unforgivable, but *The Sound and the Fury* blames none of the Compsons for being who and what—for overwhelming cultural reasons—they had to become.

Realizing that *Flags* would never see the light of day (at least in his lifetime—it was finally published a decade after his death, in 1973), Faulkner spoke of a door being closed. Finally, he thought, he could write wholly for himself. He would long remember the ecstasy he felt during the composition of *The Sound and the Fury*. He literally did not know, day by day, what was coming on the next page. All he was sure of was that it would be fresh, right, and entirely his own. He never expected the book to be published, but when Hal Smith surprisingly said yes, a masterwork appeared. Few critics had a clue about what to make of this extraordinary novel. However, one reviewer, Evelyn Scott, grasped what Faulkner had wrought: "Here is beauty sprung from the perfect *realization* of what a more limiting morality would describe as ugliness," she wrote. "Here is a humanity stripped of what was claimed for it by the Victorians, and the spectacle is moving as no sugar-coated drama could ever be."

As I Lay Dying followed *The Sound and the Fury*. Written in barely seven weeks, it is even leaner and more jagged. The novel centers on something one might think beyond fiction's capacity to say: "that pride, that furious desire to hide that abject nakedness which we bring here with us . . . carry stubbornly with us into the earth again." It probes the barriers we draw on to conceal our psychic nakedness from others; it also grasps the distress that occurs when those barriers are breached. Many of the book's 59 chapters articulate the self's imprisoning inwardness. Oddly enough, this is an inwardness experienced even in the presence of others: Addie Bundren, the dead mother, had felt her imprisonment inside herself the most keenly. Her awareness (earlier, as a teacher) of her students "each with his and her secret and selfish thought" drove her wild. She would whip them with a switch, thinking with each blow, "Now you are aware of me! Now I am something in your secret and selfish life, who have marked your blood with my own for ever and ever." Mere words between teacher and students could not cross this divide. "We had had to use one another by words like spiders dangling by their mouths from a beam, swinging and twisting and never touching, and that only through the blows of the switch could my blood and their blood flow as one stream."

Words that swing and twist and never touch are no good. They do not reach the other person with their force intact, and they fail to penetrate the pride-installed boundaries that protect each self's lifelong nakedness. What is needed are words that hurt and break through the self's defenses. Addie's insulated husband, Anse, will go to his grave unmarked and virginal (despite his having fathered four children). He has remained cradled throughout his life, thanks to the cottony protection of the words he lives within and takes to be real.

The Sound and the Fury was Faulkner's first novel to hew its way into "wordless" territory. In it, he twisted syntax and procedure with unprecedented violence; in doing so, he charged that novel with something rarely seen before: it enacts (like *As I Lay Dying*) less a saying that goes into the air than a doing that "goes along the earth." It seeks not to entertain or deliver truths, but aims to penetrate the reader's heart.

With these two novels behind him, the even starker *Sanctuary* appeared in 1931. It is no surprise that these three back-to-back books catapulted Faulkner into fame and recognition as America's most powerful novelist. Never again would Faulkner write the drama of stumbling with more brutal force. *Sanctuary* became notorious, and it would remain, throughout his life, the one novel that pigeonholed his identity. For countless people who never even read the book, it established Faulkner as the "corn-cob man," because they thought *Sanctuary* centered on the horrific corncob rape of its main character, Temple Drake. The fact that this scene is all but undiscoverable in the published novel mattered little to those who hadn't read it anyway. But for Faulkner, completing the book posed a unique challenge.

He had conceived it in 1928 as a potboiler, a story based on the most lurid plot he could imagine—"a cheap idea," as he liked to call it. After reading the manuscript, his friend and editor, Hal Smith, was sure that the book was unpublishable. If they released it, Smith told Faulkner, "We'll both be in jail." But, for unknown reasons, Smith changed his mind in 1931, and Faulkner suddenly received the galleys. This half-forgotten novel—started before *The Sound and the Fury* or *As I Lay Dying*, and dropped from sight for two years—was now going to see the light. Faulkner was aghast at what the galleys for *Sanctuary* revealed. He had in the interim become a different writer, so how could he publish *Sanctuary* without tarnishing the achievement he had wrought in the previous two masterpieces? His answer was to revise it thoroughly, and entirely at his own expense.

The resulting novel is perhaps the one that sparks the most disagreements among Faulkner's critics and readers alike. French critics were the first to celebrate *Sanctuary*. And they were not just *any* French critics, but some of the most revered names in 20th-century Western culture: Jean-Paul Sartre, André Malraux, and Albert Camus. (Malraux memorably characterized *Sanctuary* as the union of Greek tragedy and the detective novel.) It would take decades before American commentary on Faulkner caught up with their level of sophistication. Perhaps as well, a French penchant for the bleaker Faulkner has *Sanctuary* ranking so high for so long. The novel's cast of characters, at any rate, is close to unrelievedly sordid. They include a deformed underworld figure named Popeye, a senile old man named Pap, a half-wit named Tommy, and a crew of violent bootleggers. Into this mix comes, by the sheer misfortune of a car accident, a drunken young Oxford man as pretentious as he is out of his depth. And with him, his unfortunate date, the flirtatious young Ole Miss undergraduate (and the daughter of a judge), Temple Drake. At Frenchman's Bend (where the bootleggers carry out their trade), surrounded by these lawless men, she will meet her fate. Here is how Faulkner writes her distress:

> She snatched it [her hand] up with a wailing shriek, clapping it against her mouth, and turned and ran toward the door. The woman caught her arm . . . and Temple sprang back into the kitchen. . . . "Let go," she whispered,

"let go! Let go!" She surged and plunged, grinding the woman's hand against the door jamb until she was free. She sprang from the porch and ran toward the barn . . . Then suddenly she ran upside down in a rushing interval; she could see her legs still running in space, and she struck lightly and solidly on her back and lay still . . . Her hand moved in the substance in which she lay, then she remembered the rat . . . Her whole body surged in an involuted spurning movement . . . so that she flung her hands out and caught herself upright . . . her face not twelve inches from the cross beam on which the rat crouched. For an instant they stared eye to eye, then its eyes glowed suddenly like two tiny electric bulbs and it leaped at her head just as she sprang backward, treading again on something that rolled under her foot. She fell toward the opposite corner, on her face in the hulls and a few scattered corn-cobs gnawed bone-clean . . . Then she got to her feet and sprang at the door . . . rasping at the planks with her bare hands.

This entire passage registers the ongoing rape of Temple, hours before the actual incident occurs. None of the material surfaces near her accommodate contact with her body: kitchen door and barn door, the other woman's hand, her own hand, her own legs, and scattered corn-cobs (for the moment harmless). These entities seem wired, gone awry, capable of "rasping" her. Charged with hostility, they align with the rat. As in a nightmare, the rat that is glimpsed will next be only 12 inches from Temple's face. It stares at her as though it knows her; then it leaps. As in a nightmare, she can escape nothing that enters her space.

The power of *Sanctuary* lodges in passages such as this. Faulkner cannot take his eye off what is being done to Temple at Frenchman's Bend. Layer after layer, the sanctuaries that protect her identity are stripped away. The assault is both bodily and psychological. "My father's a judge," she wails, as she seeks to smile, cringe, or fantasize her way back into security. Her defenses are ripped from her, and—hooked on booze and riddled with lust—she becomes, for the last third of the book, a denizen of the Memphis underworld. She has traded Daddy (her father the judge) for "Daddy" (Popeye). Impotent himself, he makes orgasmic, whinnying noises as he stands by her bed. As though mesmerized, he watches her writhe in intercourse with his delegated substitute, Red. Waiting for Red, Temple "felt long shuddering waves of physical desire going over her, draining the color from her mouth, drawing her eyeballs back into her skull in a shuddering swoon." Her drawn-back eyeballs recall the rat's glowing ones. Living creatures are accessed as body parts enlivened by instinct; they surge and glow, and "She could tell all of them by the way they breathed." The human world, stripped of its sanctuaries, transforms into a barnyard.

Sanctuary joined As I Lay Dying as a sort of narrative experiment in how much pressure people can bear. In both novels, Faulkner submits the habits and pieties of his central figures to an all-but-apocalyptic assault. These include flood and fire in the one novel and the underworld of Frenchman's Bend and Memphis in the other. He does this to discover what, under the impress of that assault, those figures will become. With almost inhuman detachment, he experiments with his characters, pushing them past the conditions that sustain their coherence, making them stumble out of their familiar identity.

It is a short step to move from "almost inhuman" and arrive at "misogynistic." Many readers—offended by the abuse inflicted on Temple—take that step. Some of the abuse Temple endures supports such a reading. The novel indulges in recurrent sneers about Temple's privilege, dilating on her ignorance of everything outside her family's genteel, protected world. To that extent, Sanctuary can be seen as committed to "teaching her a lesson." Yet, Temple learns no lesson. The book is darker than any pedagogic purpose can illuminate. "It's like there was a fellow in every man," Cash Bundren thinks at the conclusion of As I Lay Dying, "that's done a-past the sanity or the insanity, that watches the sane and the insane doings of that man with the same horror and the same astonishment." Temple reveals such sanity/insanity as she is being raped:

> Then I said That wont do. I ought to be a man. So I was an
> old man, with a long white beard, and then the little black
> man got littler and littler and I was saying Now. You see

now. I'm a man now. Then I thought about being a man, and as soon as I thought it, it happened. It made a kind of plopping sound, like blowing a little rubber tube wrong-side outward. It felt cold, like the inside of your mouth when you hold it open. I could feel it, and I lay right still to keep from laughing about how surprised he was going to be. I could feel the jerking going inside my knickers ahead of his hand and me lying there trying not to laugh about how surprised and mad he was going to be in a minute.

In this passage, we encounter Temple's trauma itself. Faulkner doesn't narrate it; rather, he makes it speak. The fantasy-narrative it speaks both reveals and conceals the assault she is undergoing. We see everything materially relevant—the corncob, the invaded body, the jerking flesh. But we see it fantastically reconfigured. That is, we see the crazily cross-gendered scenario that her defenses have summoned into being if she is to survive the rape. In *The Sound and the Fury*, Quentin fantasized himself as Dalton Ames's mother in a scene of intercourse. He imagined her withdrawing her husband's penis before ejaculation, thus killing Ames before he was conceived. No less bizarrely, Temple has fantasized herself onto an impossible stage. Won't Popeye be surprised, she now thinks, to discover she has become an old man with a long white beard? Faulkner dwells less on what is done to Temple than on what she frantically does with what is done to her.

Her doing is psychic alone because there is no other way of escaping Popeye. He co-opts material reality; she absents herself through psychic fantasy. The poetry of this passage is the poetry of Temple's outraged system of defenses. Inasmuch as the defenses are there to prevent such outrage, Faulkner's prose finds its way to Temple's very core. With horror and astonishment, we hear her psyche speak. What it speaks is no barnyard, no release of animal instinct. It speaks a kind of pain that only human beings, on the rack, are capable of.

Faulkner called this novel a cheap idea, a potboiler. His critics looked deeper and glimpsed the psychological insights of Fyodor Dostoevsky. Faulkner claimed not to have read the Russian author's books, but he said that about a lot of writers. Secret sharers—the term is Joseph Conrad's, a writer Faulkner never disowned—were his imaginative company. His great work penetrates beneath the sanctuaries that sustain identity. It undoes those conceptual bulwarks within which we can claim that we are thus and so, and not otherwise. Exerting strong pressure, these novels come upon unspeakable transformations. It is as though, deep down, humans were alterable plasma rather than fixed essence. The one who writes a misogynistic potboiler—a man who sees his difference from a woman as absolute, who narratively abuses her and believes she deserves what she gets—is the corn-cob man. But the one who stages the nightmarish transferences that stalk our daytime identities is a genius. They are both Faulkner, and it took them both to write *Sanctuary*.

The novel was published in February 1931. On a personal front, it was a difficult time for Faulkner and Estelle. The previous year they had moved into a new home, Rowan Oak, and were now expecting a child. But the pregnancy had been difficult, and the baby was born two months early, on an icy night in January 1931. They named her Alabama, after his beloved great-aunt, but the tiny infant was immediately sick and she worsened steadily. Despite every move the desperate Faulkner could think of—including a feverish search for an incubator impossible to locate outside of Memphis—Alabama died 10 days later. The weakened and hospitalized Estelle never saw her child alive.

Once more, Faulkner recognized his powerlessness before the assault of *is*—as though his infant's irreversible decline stayed mockingly in advance of any counter-measures he could cobble together. Alabama would haunt him later; her unlived possibilities would appear to him as uncannily prefigured in the earlier genesis of his heart's darling, Caddy Compson. "So I, who never had a sister," he wrote in a 1933 preface to *The Sound and the Fury*, "and was fated to lose my daughter in infancy, set out to make myself a beautiful and tragic little girl." The peace of *was*, the turmoil of *is*. He had been unable to save his daughter during the assault of *is*. But he repossessed her imaginatively and retrospectively, yet in advance of her actual birth. Aligning his dead baby with his immortal Caddy, he bestowed on her (in that 1933 preface) a fullness of meaning she could not have possessed that dark day in January 1931.

Estelle remained weak that entire spring and into the summer as well. Faulkner badly needed money to keep his household intact; he had already missed the March mortgage payment. In droves, he began to submit short stories to the national journals. The rejection letters came back, also in droves. Then something different arrived in the mail. Professor James Wilson of the University of Virginia wrote to invite him to a conference of Southern writers, to be held in Charlottesville later that year. The conference had been instigated by the novelist Ellen Glasgow and was supported by notables such as writers Thomas Wolfe, Paul Green, and Sherwood Anderson, philosopher Donald Davidson, and poet Allen Tate. Its aim was to shed light on the recent flourishing of Southern letters. *Sanctuary* had been published in February 1931, to a flurry of critical responses. *The Sound and the Fury* and *As I Lay Dying* had appeared shortly before that. The latter was now lined up for translation into French. Faulkner had become pretty hard to ignore, and the conference organizers wanted him to be among their 34 attendees. He responded to their invitation with a letter that revealed his misgivings even while agreeing to participate:

Dear Mr Wilson—

Thank you for your invitation. I would like very much to avail myself of it, what with your letter's pleasing assurance that loopholes will be supplied to them who have peculiarities about social gambits. You have seen a country wagon come into town, with a hound dog under the wagon. It stops on the Square and the folks get out, but that hound never gets very far from that wagon. He might be cajoled or scared out for a short distance, but first thing you know he has scuttled back under the wagon; maybe he growls at you a little. Well, that's me . . .

He was apprehensive when he arrived in Charlottesville. Apparently his first words to his host were, "Know where I can get a drink?" Since Prohibition was still in effect, the host took him to his own bootleg supplier. Cushioned by a bottle of corn whiskey, the two of them spent a convivial evening together. But as the conference got under way, things spiraled out of control. Faulkner appeared at the first meeting wearing what Paul Green took to be an aviator's cap. Swiftly he became the focal point of the conference. His response to this unwonted attention was to hit the bottle even more aggressively. "Bill Faulkner had arrived and got drunk," Sherwood Anderson later reported. Allen Tate recalled Faulkner's asking Tate's wife where he could get another drink, then vomiting on her dress. His friends knew he had to be extricated, and soon. Paul Green and Hal Smith got him into a car and drove him to New York. Faulkner seems to have been steadily drinking the whole time. As they passed through Washington, D.C., he invited a policeman they crossed on the street to join them for yet another tipple. On October 26, they finally arrived in New York.

An unbearable posse of attention was waiting for him. Harold Guinzburg of Viking, Alfred Knopf of Knopf, and Bennett Cerf of Random House were there, each determined to sign him up. Faced with all this attention, Faulkner became even more anxious and stepped up the drinking. During these two weeks, he was out of control. When the actress Tallulah Bankhead begged him to do a screenplay for her, he wrote Estelle: "The contract is to be signed today, for about $10,000." (Nothing ever came of this project.) A couple of days later he wrote Estelle again: "I have created quite a sensation . . . In fact, I have learned with astonishment that I am now the most important figure in American letters."

In fact, "astonishment" and inebriation seem to have characterized the six weeks of Faulkner's frantic, alcohol-fueled stay in New York. Once he had met Lillian Hellman, Dashiell Hammett, and Nathaniel West, he was surrounded by a peerless crew of fellow boozers. He was passing out in public places frequently enough for Hal Smith to contact Faulkner's friend Ben Wasson for help. Wasson urged Estelle to come up quickly to New York and rescue her husband; she took the train and arrived at the beginning of December. But her presence seemed to add fuel to the fire rather than calm things down. Bennett Cerf remembered her standing at the window of his apartment on Central Park South, at one of his parties. She remarked on the beauty of the view outside, saying to him: "I feel just like throwing myself out the window." Cerf was alarmed: "Oh, Estelle, you don't mean that." She stared at him and said, "*Of course I do.*" Writer Dorothy Parker spoke of Estelle's ripping her dress and attempting to leap out the window of Parker's Algonquin Hotel rooms. Another of their new acquaintances, playwright Marc Connelly, remembered her losing control at a social gathering one night. Faulkner was next to her, engaged in conversation, when he noticed what was happening. With no expression on his face, he reached out and slapped her, very hard. She returned immediately to normal, and he continued his conversation.

This whirlwind outburst of manic behavior lasted from late October to mid-December of 1931. Faulkner had long been a heavy drinker, but something newly disturbing seemed to emerge during the University of Virginia fiasco. "You know that state I seem to get into when people come to see me and I begin to visualize a kind of jail corridor of literary talk," he wrote a friend about the conference debacle. Earlier, we recall, he had viewed his approaching and inescapable marriage with Estelle as a sort of "jail corridor." But the reasons for this later feeling of claustrophobia were different: Faulkner could not forget that—however deliberately—he had not gone past the 11th grade, so he had no business speaking to these literary people. He required silence for his sanity and to get his work done. His intense bond with his books was speechlessly enacted in writing them, not in talking about them later. He may have sought the widest recognition, but more than that, viscerally, he was a hound dog that wanted to stay scuttled under the wagon. Is it any wonder that his greatest fiction—including the three novels that launched the New York frenzy—centers on the unpreparedness experienced during moments of crisis? The assault of what you are not ready for, the outrage of *is*? This rhythm of stumbling marked his life and it marks his greatest fiction as well.

3

Flight and Fall

The romance of flight began early. The Wright brothers—starting with nothing and ending with the grand prize—had been enshrined as American heroes. As a kid, Faulkner had persuaded his siblings to build their own aircraft. They used rotten wood, rusty nails, grocery bags, wrapping paper, and a design taken from a boys' magazine. After several weeks, William decided to give the plane its trial run. The collapse that followed eerily foreshadowed some subsequent attempts to take to the air.

As his brother John would later recall, at about the same time there was another airborne adventure. At one of the local fairs, the most spectacular stunt involved the exploits of a scruffy self-proclaimed airman. This fellow would arrive on the scene already drunk, carrying a parachute and a huge canvas bag. The plan was to fill the bag with hot air to the point where, with him attached below, it would rise into the air. While the bag was filling, the airman steadily cursed and clamored for more booze, his eyes red and streaming, thanks to the smoke and flames. Once the balloon seemed ready, its inebriated passenger would fasten his parachute harness and strap himself in. By the time the balloon started its climb, the Falkner boys' excitement would be beyond containing. They ran at full speed, following the airborne balloon, hoping to see the pilot make his escape. They came upon him minutes later, already on the ground and so drunk that he hardly felt the violence of his abortive landing. Drink, grease, cursing, and desperate risk: Faulkner may from the beginning have carried these associations with the human attempt to fly. They were probably revivified during the 1930s when he avidly watched scruffy barnstorming flyers perform their daredevil stunts at county fairs—the years prior to his writing *Pylon*.

In 1918, his only alternative to Estelle's marriage to Franklin had been a protracted attempt to fight in the Great War. Whether that would be made possible in America or Canada, Faulkner invariably insisted on joining the Air Force. The letters RAF (Royal Air Force) would remain a precious acronym he never tired of mentioning. His five months of flight training in Canada not only gave him material for a number of stories and, at least, four novels, but they also nurtured his fascination with the mechanics of flight—with the fragile and murderous beauty of aircraft. He could not get enough of the planes, and his sketches of them were exquisitely precise. What most drew him to these flying machines, it seems, was their apparent weightlessness. They were mere "kites" constructed of wood and canvas and wire, powered by untrustworthy engines. Soon Faulkner could distinguish expertly among the different military craft at the air base, and he was writing home to his mother of solo flights. These vignettes would later expand—balloonistically—into more high-flying fantasy. Flights, crashes, and injuries: he asserted all of these with great energy, though no evidence supports the claims.

As early as 1919, Faulkner was squirming over his flying predicament. "Everybody thinks I can fly, but I can't," he told a pilot friend at the University of Mississippi. The only remedy was to take lessons on the sly, off and on for the next decade. As soon as he expected bigger money to come his way—royalties anticipated from the notorious *Sanctuary* (1931)—he returned to the flying project. Vernon Omlie, a professional instructor, taught him all spring of 1933. The training took place in Omlie's powerful Waco F biplane. Faulkner lifted off for his first solo flight on April 20 of that year. By the fall, he was confident enough of his abilities to purchase Omlie's Waco at the considerable cost—for the time—of $6000. Considering that three years earlier he had paid the same amount to purchase his home, Rowan Oak, and its four acres, we get a measure of how far he would go to indulge his flying obsession. Faulkner adored this plane, and it elicited one of the rare photos of him smiling that exists. In it, he's grinning broadly, his hand extended possessively toward his Waco as though it were a precious object he had never believed he might own.

The subsequent step seemed obvious. He wanted his three younger brothers to become as passionate about flying as he was. That turned out to be easy, and soon enough—barnstorming together across several counties—they were collectively known as "the flying Falkners." Not long thereafter, it became clear to Faulkner that his youngest brother Dean, though unable to support himself financially, was the most talented flyer of them all. Faulkner adored this youngest sibling, and Dean reciprocated the feeling. He even cultivated a thin mustache that resembled Faulkner's, and he added a "u" to his name so as to tighten their bond. So Faulkner sold Dean the Waco, at a price so low as to make it virtually a gift. The transaction apparently worked. Dean married the woman he had been engaged to and began to earn a decent living giving flying lessons.

Flying was on Faulkner's mind in other ways as well. In the fall of 1934, he suddenly began to write—at breakneck speed—a new novel, *Pylon*. It was devoted to the madness of barnstormers scrapping to make a living high in the air. He completed his manuscript in just two months because, one supposes, the larger challenge of dominating the air had been on his mind for years. He had grown up seeing daredevils risking hot-air balloon rides at the carnivals of his childhood. Before, during, and after his RAF stint in Toronto during the war years, he was fascinated with airplanes; in 1935, *Pylon* was born out of this obsession.

Linguistically, it is Faulkner's most extravagant novel. Its sentences burst at their seam, as though they were land-constrained, striving to rise into the air. Of the planes themselves Faulkner wrote:

> Creatures imbued with motion though not with life and incomprehensible to the puny crawling painwebbed globe, incapable of suffering, wombed and born complete and instantaneous, cunning intricate and deadly, from out some blind iron batcave of the earth's prime foundation.

The source of his fascination with flying leaps off the page here: the inhuman power of the planes. They pulse with capacities that mock self-imposed human limits. They transcend conventions erected to make life safe, organized, mutual. Free of the messiness of human attachment (life on the "painwebbed globe"), they beam forth sheer autonomous speed.

The pilots who fly them, drunk on such speed, have abandoned all calculations that sustain life on the land. As one of the pilots says about the races in *Pylon*, "And the ship is all right, except you won't know until you are in the air whether or not you can take it off and you won't know until you are back on the ground and standing up again whether or not you can land it." You also won't know if you'll survive until afterward. No preparation is any good. So much for plans to master life in time, to calculate before and after. To fly those "kites" was to experience time as pure presence.

"Breathing is a sight-draft dated yesterday," Faulkner's character, Will Varner, later claimed in *The Hamlet* (1940), the first novel of Faulkner's Snopes family trilogy. His words imply that our breath has a possible liquidation date of "yesterday" written on it—it is collectible on sight. Our final exit could be any time, and there will likely be no notice. Nothing brought home this dimension of life's uninsurable tenure more powerfully than flying. In its intrinsic risk Faulkner must have recognized its hypnotic appeal: the dance with death itself. Is that why, after hearing in June 1934 of the famous pilot Jimmy Wedell's fatal crash, he deemed the moment right for writing his own will? Wedell had crashed while giving a beginner flight lessons. But how would this event—how would anyone else's disaster—have prepared him for the airborne nightmare hurtling toward him?

The Waco biplane deal with Dean seemed too good to be true, and it was. One day in late 1935, after Dean had taken up a group of student-passengers in the Waco, he failed to return. Rumors of a crash spread. Late that afternoon Faulkner got the dreaded call. The plane had crashed, and Dean was dead. The Waco had been found, buried six feet under the earth; all the bodies were mutilated beyond recognition. That night, Faulkner did not allow other family members to approach the mangled corpse of his brother. Carrying a photo of Dean with him, he worked with the undertaker for hours, recomposing a face that might pass for Dean's. What atonement was Faulkner enacting during this gruesome ritual? Likely it was a mix of family piety (make Dean presentable again for his mother and his wife), self-inflicted torture (it was his Waco, hence his fault), and the painstaking inscription of a life-long memory (Dean's ruined face to remain forever inside him). The accident was never fully explained, though experts believed one of the passengers had been given the controls and had put the plane into a fatal spin.

No one was officially to blame, yet Faulkner could not forgive himself for what had happened. His love of flying, his Waco, Dean's death: he kept asking himself how to explain that sequence? Later, a tear-wracked Faulkner told Dean's grieving widow Louise, "I've ruined your life. It's all my fault." A few weeks after that, at breakfast one morning, Louise said, "I can't eat. I dreamed the whole accident last night." Faulkner responded, "You're lucky to have dreamed it only once. I dream it every night."

In this state of mind, Faulkner played and replayed the events that had shaped his identity: the woman he had not eloped with, the war he had not entered, and the plane he had secretly been incapable of flying. Each of these had multiple, incompatible lives over time. Each had escaped him at first. Each had then become an intricate part of his life. The first and the last would break his heart. Along with Estelle's marriage to Cornell Franklin, Dean's death was the worst thing that had ever happened to him. It would haunt him for the rest of his life.

4

"Go slow now"

"Go slow now": this is probably Faulkner's most quoted (and notorious) remark about race. Addressed publicly to black leaders, it expressed his heartfelt desire to avoid yet further racial violence. In 1954, the Supreme Court had made its game-changing decision in the case of Brown vs. the Board of Education. The judges determined that the doctrine of "separate but equal" (until then, the law of the land on matters of race) could no longer stand. Separate was not equal, and racial integration would be the new mandate. Faulkner did not dispute the ruling. What he feared was the cataclysm of violence that would follow any federal attempts to turn law into Southern reality.

"Go slow now" articulates Faulkner's abiding concern about the civil rights agitation of the 1950s. The two races—at least in his beloved South—were nowhere near ready to integrate. He was urging blacks to recognize this cardinal fact on the ground—and to slow down their campaign for integration accordingly. Yet, the phrase captures only the negative half of Faulkner's richly tortured understanding of race. The fuller picture requires us to draw on another of his phrases, one less often cited but perhaps even more revealing: "dark twins."

That phrase appears in Faulkner's second novel, *Mosquitoes*. There, he used it to characterize the intricate bond between an author's life and his work: "A book is a writer's secret life, the dark twin of a man: you can't reconcile them." Unlike "go slow now," "dark twins" suggests Faulkner's abiding twinship with blacks, along with his no less abiding difference from them. The dark face he (as a Southerner) sees in the mirror proposed by race cannot be his own. Yet, recurrently, he cannot avoid glimpsing himself there as well. More broadly, for several centuries in the South, the two races were both intertwined and cordoned off. They were at once inseparable and irreconcilable, scandalously connected by mixed blood, yet segregated by law. Most of Faulkner's countrymen denied the twinship, insisting instead on unbridgeable differences. But Faulkner found himself caught in a weave of racial realities he could neither master nor escape. He moved through this territory uncertainly, careening between blindness and insight. He knew at once too much and not enough. A rehearsal of his contradictory speeches during the civil rights turmoil of the 1950s reveals this all too clearly.

As a considerably inebriated Faulkner told journalist Russell Howe, "If I have to choose between the United States government and Mississippi, then I'll choose Mississippi. . . . [I]f it came to fighting I'd fight for Mississippi against the United States even if it meant going out into the street and shooting Negroes." The interview took place in New York in March 1956, when civil rights turmoil was at a boiling point. A young black woman named Autherine Lucy had been accepted into the University of Alabama. Southerners were rioting at the prospect, but a federal court ordered the University to admit her nevertheless. Faulkner thought she would not enter the university alive and pleaded for caution. Word of his desire to speak got out and *The Reporter* sent Howe to interview Faulkner. But when the interview appeared in print, Faulkner was horrified by his own words. He immediately wrote a letter to *The Reporter* explaining that the statements attributed to him were ones "which no sober man would make, nor . . . any sane man believe." Aghast, he felt betrayed by the mirror image of his own quoted voice. A month later he would claim that Howe's interview was "more a misconstruction than a misquotation." He conceded that these were his words, but not his thoughts. Something more than incoherence was at work in his sense of self-betrayal.

Repeatedly (as "go slow now" suggests), the default pole in Faulkner's racial stance was "disidentification." He could not be his dark twin. One cannot imagine his uttering the phrase, "shooting whites," no matter how drunk. Somewhere inside his psyche, nurtured by his region's racial convictions, he *could* envisage shooting Negroes.

His words to Howe further reveal his blindness toward black lives. If it came to violence, he insisted, "My Negro boys down on the plantation would fight against the North with me. If I say to them, 'Go get your shotguns, boys,' they'll come." The master/slave model was clear: he was the man, and they were the boys; he gave the orders, they obeyed. This widely shared fantasy failed the South in the Civil War when black slaves—given the chance—fled in huge numbers from their Southern masters. The fantasy was outrageous when sounded in 1956.

Autherine Lucy's admission to the University of Alabama was legal and unstoppable. But "go slow now" meant: be careful, be realistic. "You have the power now," Faulkner wrote to the black leaders, but it is a power to be restrained. Some of his other race-focused statements made it clear that he meant *really* slow. About the change sanctioned by *Brown* he opined: "That will take a little time . . . the Negro himself has got to be patient and sensible. But it will come, as I see it, and maybe in three hundred years." (Elsewhere he would speak of 500 years.) He was urging a pace of political change that could only appear to black leaders as glacial.

For him, it was the *white* South that was at risk. At a Southern Historical Association conference in Memphis in 1955, he said the following: "We will not sit quietly by and see our native land, the South, not just Mississippi but all the South, wreck and ruin itself twice in less than a hundred years, over the Negro question." In private correspondence, he was more colloquial. "For the second time in a hundred years," he wrote to a concerned Mississippian, "we Southerners will have destroyed our native land just because of niggers." That phrasing sticks in the craw. But Faulkner's thinking seems to have been: "Why won't they be patient, wait out a change in white behavior and politics that is overdue but will in time arrive?"

White hearts could not be forced to change, but black hearts, Faulkner wanted to believe, might be more alterable. Integration might become feasible if blacks ceased to be, well, *black*. During his year of teaching at the University of Virginia (1957-1958), he pronounced the following: "Perhaps the Negro is not yet capable of more than second-class citizenship. His tragedy may be that so far he is competent for equality only in the ratio of his white blood. . . . He must learn to cease forever more thinking like a Negro and acting like a Negro. . . . His burden will be that, because of his race and color, it will not suffice him to think and act like just any white man: he must think and act like the best among white men." Even as Faulkner conceded here a history of miscegenation, it was only to imagine its (unintended) benefits for blacks. More, just as white brutality was erased from this vision of miscegenation, it was also omitted in his insistence that black behavior be equal to the *best* of white behavior.

The same distortions had appeared a year earlier, when he urged black leaders to say to their followers, "We must learn to deserve equality so that we can hold and keep it after we get it." *Deserve equality*: Faulkner's phrasing rejected Thomas Jefferson's insistence on equality as a self-evident truth in no need of "deserving." Not so for blacks, however. Faulkner would mortgage their equality to demonstrated proofs of merit. Missing from these utterances was the capacity to enter empathically into black lives. He could not envisage those lives as already precious and in need of support on their own terms. For him, in statements such as this one, there would be no equality for blacks until they looked—and smelled—more like whites: he advised black leaders to tell their people to "let us practice cleanliness . . . in our contacts with" the white man. If such obtuseness about racial turmoil were the last word concerning Faulkner's dark twinship, there would be much darkness and little twinning. That was how most black leaders and white radicals understood his pronouncements. Not surprisingly, they expected little from this famous white Southerner.

"Even if it means going out into the street and shooting Negroes," Faulkner had said in 1956. It may be hard in the 21st century to recall the race-fueled violence that used to blanket the Southern landscape like immovable summer heat. Here is "testimony" from Memphis—not only a city near Oxford that Faulkner knew well, but also widely recognized then as "Murder Capital" of America. The bulk of Memphis's routine violence was racial, so much so that the *Commercial Appeal* (the main Memphis newspaper and the one to which Faulkner often wrote letters to the Editor) thought fit (in 1906) to exhort its readership as follows: "This thing of killing negroes without cause . . . [is being] overdone . . . white men who kill negroes as a pastime . .

. usually end up killing white men." The norms running through this editorial—and newspapers survive only by shared norms—testify to the unthinking entrenchment of Southern racism. The editorial assumes that all readers of the paper are white, it envisages whites killing blacks as an "overdone . . . pastime." The disturbing consequence of such a foolish practice is that white men could end up getting killed.

Indeed, at the beginning of the 20th century, lynchings of black people were so numerous as to appear almost common. Faulkner claimed he had never witnessed one, and there is no reason to doubt him. But Mississippi led the nation in lynchings during this period. As historian Joel Williamson has noted, "In the twenty years from 1889 to 1909, at least 293 blacks were lynched there, more than in any other state in the nation." One of the most notorious lynchings—that of Nelse Patton—occurred in Oxford in 1908. Patton was thought to have murdered a woman named Mattie McMillan with a razor blade. He fled the scene but was soon caught by outraged whites. Williamson has shown how journalists and politicians fed the flames of the ensuing racial fury. First reported as "a white woman," Mattie was within hours referred to as "a white lady." At first, she was "killed," but within hours, the papers reported her as "assaulted and killed." Furious Oxford residents caught Patton and stubbornly prevented the law from taking its course. Brick by brick, they tore down the symbolic courthouse to get at Patton and remove him from the protections guaranteed by the law. They riddled his body with bullets and strung him up naked and mutilated on a telephone pole. His body remained on display all night. Ten-year-old William Faulkner slept only 1,000 yards from the courthouse that night. He didn't have to witness this ritual dismembering to remember its impact for the rest of his life.

I have cast Faulkner's immersion in American race relations as oscillating between blindness and insight, disidentification and identification. His twinship with blacks remained dark, but it could become, at times, radiant. When it did so, the source of his perceptiveness was likely to have been his childhood nurse and protectress, Mammy Callie. Indeed, she may have wielded as formative an influence on Faulkner and his brothers as their mother had. By most reports, she was more affectionate and more easily lovable than

Maud. Like black maids throughout the early 20-century South, she would have cared for his bodily needs. She would have touched him, soothed him, protected him, and—when needed—scolded him. One suspects the presence of a possible screen memory behind his earlier reference to his great-aunt's daughters Vannye and Natalie: "Vannye was impersonal; quite aloof: she was holding the lamp. Natalie was quick and dark. She was touching me. She must have carried me." Were these sisters stand-ins for Faulkner's memories of Maud and Callie?

The memoirs of his two brothers repeatedly testify to the strength of their bond with Callie. She regaled the boys with stories of the Civil War and of her childhood in slavery before it. She introduced them to the nomenclature of natural phenomena. Under her tutelage, they learned the variety of plants and animals, their specific names and habits and needs. The boys absorbed as well the folktales that go with the flora and fauna, providing bonding narratives between human and natural worlds. Callie had entered Faulkner's parents' household in 1902, in Oxford. She played a crucial role in Faulkner's maturation from the age of five, and she would remain an emotional fixture in his life until her death almost 40 years later. She would spend her last decade in Faulkner's household. He could not imagine his daughter Jill growing up without her tutelage, as precious for her as it had been for him. "Mammy Callie was probably the most important person in his life," Jill would say to one of his biographers. Even if we discount this claim, Callie figured centrally in the formation of Faulkner's emotions and beliefs.

Faulkner has been much praised—and, by a smaller number, called into question—for pronouncing the eulogy at Callie's funeral in 1940. I am among that smaller number who have wondered in print what was at stake in his taking over that role. So it seems appropriate to cite my reasons: "Presiding over her funeral," I wrote 20 years ago, "Faulkner emphasized Callie's 'half century of fidelity and devotion,' and he went on to identify her as one of his 'earliest recollections, not only as a person, but as a fount of authority over my conduct and of security for my physical welfare, and of active and constant affection and love.' On her tombstone, he had these words written: 'Her white children bless her.' It detracts nothing from the sincerity of this engraving to note, at the same time, that the white Faulkner has taken over the roles of both wounded subject and grateful offspring, organizer of her funeral and spokesman of the grief her death caused others. In none of this do we register the reality of her own black culture, the friends and relatives who likewise (and surely with equal intensity) suffered her loss."

So I wrote then, and I do not recant these claims now. Yet, I wonder if this is straining the ethics of racial behavior a bit excessively. Perhaps the question is unanswerable or at any rate, it has no right answer. Why must we pass judgment on Faulkner's love of Callie? I proposed earlier that, though taught to register her as black and different, he could not but know that she was warm and "same." Perhaps no love is innocent, and one that crosses the membrane of race is certainly not. But it is still love. Writing about Faulkner and Callie now, some 20 years later, I would close with two considerations. First, according to Faulkner's biographer, Callie had asked him to deliver the eulogy when the time came. He hadn't come up with the idea on his own. Is it so hard to believe that she would want this world-famous writer who loved her to cobble together some appropriate words after her departure? Not innocent, maybe, but not hard to believe. Second, one of Faulkner's brothers said, at the time of their mother's death (1960), that Callie's rocking chair sat next to Maud's bed. It had remained there during these two decades between the death of the maid and that of the mistress. That empty rocking chair in Maud's bedroom was silently eloquent. It marked the place where an intimate member of the family used to sit and chat. It was the icon that, after Callie's death, her aging and solitary friend, Miss Maud, liked to regard through the eye of memory and love.

Faulkner's vexed relation to racial turmoil may be revealing in ways that simply "being right" could never be. Stumbling may indicate an error in judgment, but that is not all it indicates. Indeed, there may be dimensions of mid-century racial turmoil that you would have to have been there and stumbled through to grasp at all. In his 1956 "Letter to a Northern Editor," Faulkner put his finger on one of those dimensions. Neither simply for nor simply against integration, he described himself as "being in the middle." Critics have persuasively argued that the "middle" position Faulkner clung to—and which would not survive Brown vs. Board of Education—was the Southern stance of white liberalism. After *Brown*, the die was cast. You had to be for integration or against it; you could no longer seek a middle ground. So most Southern white liberals reluctantly retreated to a white moderate position. They genuinely wanted to avoid violence. But when the chips were down, they would not turn against the prerogatives of a society founded on segregation. Faulkner found himself isolated, with no shared platform to stand on. This stance reveals at once the strength and the limit of his racial understanding.

His countrymen hated not only what they took to be his posturing; many hated *him* as well. In 1951, he had publicly asserted that there was insufficient evidence to justify the death penalty for Willie McGee (a black man convicted of raping a white woman). Immediately thereafter, he was attacked as seditiously aligned with the Communists. A year earlier, he had publicly criticized a Mississippi court's decision to spare white Leon Turner from the death penalty. No one doubted that Turner had murdered three black children. Still, the jury couldn't bring themselves to execute a white man for this crime. Faulkner knew how swiftly the jurors would have decided otherwise if the race of the killer and the victims had been reversed. In a letter to *The Commercial Appeal* , he noted that Turner would be eventually released. Continuing, he predicted that Turner would at some later point murder another child, "who it is to be hoped—and with grief and despair one says it—will this time at least be of his own color."

Man in the middle. Historians are right that this was a disappearing option once *Brown* became American law. Moreover, white liberal guilt would hardly light the way to a post-civil rights future—that would take wide-scale agitation, coordinated marches, tactical confrontations, and multiple strategies. It would also take mass media coverage and, above all, it would take unflagging black leadership. Ultimately, in ways Faulkner would never understand, it would center on blacks themselves. They would be the ones to mastermind the strenuous, nation-wide campaign to emancipate themselves.

Why had Faulkner become so engaged in a cause he must have

recognized as unwinnable on his terms? Perhaps his most revealing answer came in an essay he wrote in 1954 on "Mississippi." There, in implicitly autobiographical terms, he meditated on his native land. "He was born of it and his bones will sleep in it; loving it even while hating some of it." You love what you also hate. You love it *despite* what you hate. What you hate is too deeply rooted to disappear just because you wish it would. What you hate is all too obvious: "But most of all he hated the intolerance and injustice: the lynching of Negroes not for the crimes they committed but because their skins were black."

"The middle" was where no effective racial politics in the mid-1950s could be constructed. But it was where, seeing too many competing realities to get them into a single vision, Faulkner found himself. He didn't want to be there, but the crisis was urgent. He had to engage it. Yet, in his novelistic bones, he also knew that race trouble in America wasn't going away anytime soon. No politicians could make that happen just by passing laws.

"Go slow now" meant all the reactionary things this phrase has been glossed to mean. But there was more: the national malady of racism did not allow any specific remedy to cure it once and for all. These ills had been present since the first slave ship arrived from the Middle Passage over four centuries earlier. Racial inequality was by now so enrooted in the South as to constitute a stubborn portion of American reality itself. But "go slow now" did not mean "stop." Faulkner deeply and strenuously wanted integration in the South, even as (despite his capacious imagination) he could not conceive of how it would peacefully come about. As he put away his speeches and his public letters in the later 1950s, he might have felt an immense sense of frustration and fatigue. There was so much work on race still to be done, but he lacked the heart and energy to pursue it further. And he knew no one was expecting him to do it. Could he have realized that his lasting contribution to the understanding of racial turmoil in his native land had already been done? It lay behind him, in his finest novels: *Light in August* (1932), *Absalom, Absalom!* (1936), and *Go Down, Moses* (1942) carry out Faulkner's deepest insights into his region's racial anxiety and violence.

Light in August was Faulkner's breakthrough novel about racial turmoil. It was as though he sat up in bed after a nightmare and wondered: "what would *I* feel like if I found out I was one of them?" There was no question of *them*. The novel didn't ask who—living in segregated "freedman's" districts all over the South—*they* might be. It features no empathic entry into Southern blackness; there are virtually no blacks in the novel at all. What the novel needed was something else: that the protagonist suffering from race relations "be" white. He had to be a man trapped in a weave of racial rumor about his identity at its core genetic level. He had to be unable to know what blood ran in his veins. This narrow optic brought a remarkable insight into focus. Beneath the surface confidence of Southern whites ran a racial anxiety bordering on hysteria. If a drop of black blood was thought to make a white man black, who might not unknowingly carry this toxic drop? No one could see the internal wreckage that such a drop would wreak; invisibly infected carriers might be anywhere. Such anxiety might be enough to alarm many a white man in the segregated South—especially if he had sat bolt upright at 3 am and wondered: what if I were black and didn't know it?

One might ask how racial identity could be a serious question in a novel that has virtually no black characters. Yet racial hysteria—like a bomb threat—can flare up with neither blacks nor bombs anywhere to be found. In a 1955 essay entitled "Stranger in the Village," James Baldwin shed light on the logic of this hysteria: "At the root of the American Negro problem," he wrote, "is the necessity of the American white man to find a way of living with the Negro in order to live with himself. . . . 'the Negro-in-America is a form of insanity which overtakes white men.'" Dark twins: it is as though the American white man had been surreptitiously infected with Negro-ness. Joe Christmas (*Light in August*'s central figure) is incapable of finding a way of living with the Negro in order to live with himself: he senses his dark twin living inejectably, blood-coiled, beneath his skin. How does Christmas come to believe this? And how does Faulkner narrate the question of Christmas's racial identity?

The first scene where we realize that Christmas may be black occurs some 70 pages into the book. Joe Brown, Christmas's white partner and cabin-sharer, is trying to explain to an angry mob of whites what he has been doing with Christmas. The latter is suspected of having slit a white woman (Joanna Burden)'s throat, set fire to her house, and fled. A thousand-dollar reward has been offered to anyone who can identify the killer, and Brown wants to collect it. The riled town, however, wants to know what Brown was doing at the scene of the fire. Another character, Byron Bunch, narrates what comes next:

> I reckon he was desperate by then. I reckon he could not only see that thousand dollars getting further away from him, but that he could begin to see somebody else getting it. . . . Because they said it was just like he had been saving what he told them next for just such a time as this. Like he had knowed that if it come to a pinch, this would save him . . . 'That's right,' he says. 'Go on. Accuse me. Accuse the white man that's trying to help you with what he knows. Accuse the white man and let the nigger go free. Accuse the white and let the nigger run.'
>
> 'Nigger?' the sheriff said. 'Nigger?'
>
> It's like he knew he had them then. Like nothing they could believe he had done would be as bad as what he could tell that somebody else had done. 'You're so smart,' he says 'The folks in this town is so smart. Fooled for three years. Calling him a foreigner for three years, when soon as I watched him three days I knew he wasn't no more a foreigner than I am. I knew before he even told me himself.' And them watching him now, and looking now and then at one another.
>
> 'You better be careful what you are saying, if it is a white man you are talking about,' the marshal says. 'I don't care if he is a murderer or not.' . .
>
> 'A nigger,' the marshal said. 'I always thought there was something funny about that fellow.'

Brown's unexpected charge, "nigger," magically reconfigures the scene. Under the cover provided by "nigger," he exits from suspicion, replaced obsessively by Christmas instead. All eyes—with previously blurred vision now corrected to 20/20—are turned on this absent figure. "Nigger" is bad enough, but what is intolerable is that none of them spotted him in advance. Belated "recognitions" click into place: "I always thought there was something funny about that fellow," the marshal says. His earlier uncertainties about Christmas have now been satisfyingly dispelled. Retrospective judgment reconfigures previous experience so that it fits ongoing prejudice. After her death, Joanna Burden—an alienated Yankee woman who lived alone in their vicinity—becomes a martyr to Southern honor, the victim of black bestiality: "Among them [were those] who believed aloud that it was an anonymous negro crime committed not by a negro but by Negro and who knew, believed, and hoped that she had been ravished too: at least once before her throat was cut and at least once afterward."

"Nigger," Faulkner shows, carries with it an entire bestial narrative. Yet, no one—not even Christmas himself—knows for sure whether he is black. The novel wryly reveals that well-founded knowledge doesn't much matter anyway. The racial identity of Joe's father—the man who impregnated his mother Milly Hines—will remain uncertain. As Byron explains to another character, the Rev. Gail Hightower, "She [Milly] told him [her father, Doc Hines] that the man was Mexican . . . Maybe that's what the fellow told the gal. But he . . . knew somehow that the fellow had nigger blood. Maybe the circus folks told him. I dont know. He aint never said how he found out, like that never made any difference. And I reckon it didn't, after the next night." It never made any difference because, after the next night, the man was dead anyway, gunned down by Hines. Inner conviction explodes into lethal action. Reliable information is academic, beside the point.

Obsessed with the boy's putative black blood, Hines has taken him to a white Memphis orphanage, where he works as a janitor. He never lets the boy out of his sight. The children at the orphanage call the strange new kid a "nigger"—not an unlikely scenario on a playground for white orphans in the early 20th-century South. And the person who is most verbally abusive is the ever-vigilant grandfather/ janitor himself. In a twist on the Calvinist God balefully scrutinizing His human subjects, Hines unceasingly *looks* Joe's racial difference into him: Hines "niggers" him—a racial penetration, from which the boy never recovers.

After being deformed by Hines, Joe is brutalized by his adoptive stepfather Simon McEachern, then betrayed by his first love, Bobbie, the waitress. Years later, at 33, Joe finds himself in Joanna Burden's house and (eventually) in her bed. As readers, we know—it is one of the first things we learn in this book—that this relationship ended two years later with Joanna's throat being slit. We have known this since the early pages. We have seen the townsfolk obscenely dilate on it, embroidering the scenario according to their racist fantasies. Yet, even though few in town doubt that the rape and murder occurred, Faulkner withholds narration of the event itself. Instead, he twice supplies the threshold scene of Joe being seated outside Joanna's door. There, coiled like a spring, he sits, listening to a far-off clock sound the hours. When it strikes midnight, he rises, thinking: "something is going to happen to me." He heads toward her house one last time. Only 200 pages later does Faulkner narrate what happens once he enters. We then become privy to what Joe and Joanna said to each other and what they did. Joanna, it turns out, had a double suicide in mind and was lying in wait for Joe with a huge, loaded revolver in her hand. Their affair was now ruined; he was not about to become a good "Negro" worker on her behalf, and she saw no other option than mutual suicide. Joe watched as she pulled the trigger point-blank, but the gun misfired. Rather than let her fire again, he reached for his knife, slit her throat, and fled. Even in Mississippi in the 1930s, a killing that transpired this way would be a case of self-defense. But like other things we learn about the real state of affairs in *Light in August*, knowing this does no good. Joe must die and undergo castration, because—in all white eyes—he is, in essence, and *therefore* in behavior, a nigger-rapist-murderer.

Although Christmas outwits his pursuers, he chooses, finally, to turn himself in. *"I am tired of running of having to carry my life like it was a basket of eggs,"* he thinks. He tries to get caught on a Friday. A day later he succeeds in getting recognized. Faulkner turns over the narrative of Christmas's recognition to an anonymous townsman, who speaks to other anonymous townsmen as follows:

He don't look any more like a nigger than I do. But it must have been the nigger blood in him. It looked like he had set out to get himself caught like a man might set out to get married. He had got clean away for a whole week. . . Then yesterday morning he come into Mottstown in broad daylight, on a Saturday with the town full of folks. He went into a white barbershop like a white man, and because he looked like a white man they never suspected him. . . . They shaved him and cut his hair and he payed them and walked out and right into a store and bought a new shirt and a tie and a straw hat . . . And then he walked the streets in broad daylight, like he owned the town, walking back and forth with people passing him a dozen times and not knowing it, until Halliday saw him and ran up and grabbed him and said, 'Aint your name Christmas?' and the nigger said that it was. He never denied it. He never did anything. He never acted like either a nigger or a white man. That was it. That was what made the folks so mad. For him to be a murderer and all dressed up and walking the town like he dared them to touch him, when he ought to have been skulking and hiding in the woods, muddy and dirty and running. It was like he never even knew he was a murderer, let along a nigger too.

A culture's racist vernacular speaks here, with great conviction. In this particular language, "niggers" are likely to be rapist-murderers who skulk and hide in the woods. They are typically dirty as well—and recognizable as such. One recalls the speeches Faulkner made 25 years later when he reminded black people that, to deserve equality, they should act, dress, and smell like white people. In *Light in August,* however, there is no place for such condescension. In 1932, the novelist imaginatively knew what the letter-writer and speaker of the 1950s seemed to have forgotten. Joe Christmas does not need to be reminded how to dress. With exquisite irony, he bestrides the town as though he owned it. A white barbershop, a new shirt and tie and hat, an unhurried stroll through Mottstown: his moves eloquently counter white racial expectations, point for point. He does not say a word;

his performance says it for him: "I look like you, perhaps better than you. I am clean and self-possessed. I enter and exit your segregated spaces—your barbershop and stores—and you do not see my difference. You do not see it because it does not physically exist. It takes you forever to catch up to me." I have invented this silent speech, yet something like it roils inside this mob of enraged whites. Inchoately, they register his insult. They grasp that he is mocking the racial conventions that underwrite their sanity. "The Negro-in-America is a form of insanity which overtakes white men," Baldwin wrote. *Light in August* was the first of Faulkner's masterpieces to express the fall-out of that insanity.

Four years later, in *Absalom, Absalom!*, Faulkner would go even further into race relations. Once again, the narrative would circulate around racial mystery. In the racially unknowable Joe Christmas, Faulkner must have recognized that he had reached pay dirt: he had created a "black" man who looked "white," may have been "white," but had been taught, viciously and continuously, that he was "black." *Absalom*'s racial drama is even more intricate. The figure at the heart of its mystery, Charles Bon, looks "white" and believes he is "white," and so does—until the novel's end—every reader. But at the end, when nearly every motive for his white brother's killing him has been explored and found wanting, only one explanation remains. However invisibly, however contrary to the thinking, feeling, and behavior of most others and himself, Charles must be black. As though working out a chemical experiment, Faulkner simply removes the role of melanin. Racial identity is not about essence, and it need have nothing to do with biological make-up. It has, instead, everything to do with social construction: how you are trained to see yourself and how others are trained to see you. A "nigger," both these novels reveal, is neither more nor less than someone treated as one. Yet, since (in the racial thinking of the time) one drop of black blood could do the trick, it is no less—and explosively—an identity any supposedly white man might carry within. Faulkner thus finds his way into his culture's foundational anxiety. The one race has for centuries abused and quarantined the other race because it is, essentially, no different from that other race. Dark twins: the rainbow palette of facial pigmentation visible throughout Faulkner's South speechlessly declares the same truth. Miscegenation—however illicit or denied—is his culture's open secret.

Faulkner would never probe racial distress more deeply than in *Absalom, Absalom!* Instead, a default pole in his imagination led him, recurrently, to scrutinize it more superficially. In his next novel about race, *The Unvanquished* (1938), he was determined to deal with cultural materials in a more amiable fashion than he did in *Absalom*. Southern courtliness reigns in the Civil War tales that make up *The Unvanquished*. The novel is replete with chivalric colonels (both Confederate and Yankee) and loyal slaves. The title itself announces the primary evasion that Faulkner's greater fiction confronts head-on. This is the illusion that, at its foundation, the South endured (and emerged from) the Civil War "unvanquished." I do not mean to say that Faulkner ever considered his South "vanquished." Rather, his great work shows it as permanently scarred, deformed, and not-victorious. As one of the characters in *Absalom* describes the post-1865 situation in the South, "They might have kilt us, but they aint whupped us yet." Note the core insight of such gallows humor: not defeated, but dead nevertheless.

In the late 1930s and early 1940s, Faulkner tried to raise money repeatedly without resorting to Hollywood (though he did occasionally work as a screenwriter for MGM Studios during this time). To do so, he sought to publish works that (like *The Unvanquished*) were easier to access. These would be novels that did not undermine (or undermined less) his Southern readers' expectations. To this end, he gathered together eight stories he had earlier published (at good prices) in a magazine form—"stories about niggers," as he casually described them to a friend. He thought these might make up a high-spirited, comic novel filled with racial shenanigans. He would give it the title of the last story in the collection, "Go Down, Moses."

The following vignette conveys something of the default tenor of race relations in *Go Down, Moses*. In his guise as a farmer who had purchased a good-sized farm in 1938, Faulkner owned a scrawny little bull called Black Buster. Uncle Ned (Faulkner's canny black worker who largely ran the farm for him) soon became fond of Black Buster. But it seems that the bull was ineffective at his designated job: impregnating cows. So Faulkner paid a hefty price for a large pedigreed bull that would get that job done. As the Fourth of July approached, Faulkner told Ned to slaughter Black Buster so that they all might, at least, get one good thing from him: tasty barbecue ribs. Ned agreed. The guests arrived, the ribs were served, and the meal was delicious. While savoring his ribs, Faulkner happened to notice Black Buster roaming in the fields. Alarmed, he turned to Ned, pointed to the bull, and asked, "Who's that?" Ned answered, "That's Black Buster." Faulkner looked at the ribs on the barbecue pit, "Then who's this? I thought I told you to kill Black Buster and I thought you told me you did." As Faulkner realized he hadn't seen his pedigree bull for a few days, Ned was backing away swiftly from the picnic space. "Master, I calls them all Black Buster," he said in retreat.

The tone here fills much of *Go Down, Moses*. Blacks may be in positions of servitude, but they are often cleverer than their masters. You give them orders, and they seem to comply. But you eventually discover that, once again, they have outwitted you. "Stories about niggers": whenever they are not kept under strict supervision, they find ways of making trouble. Indeed, they get away with mayhem, while the frustrated white landowner labors like a slave to keep them in line. Such a reactionary comic tenor—"look what they did this time!"—runs through many of the stories Faulkner was bringing together. There was no way to eliminate it altogether, so he came up with something better: he would make this tenor pay. He would squeeze out all the comedy these materials harbored, all the while en route, circuitously, toward the tragic core beneath.

"The Bear" is *Go Down, Moses*'s centerpiece—a hunting story that has few equals in American literature. It centers, through the perspective of young Ike McCaslin, on the immemorial ceremony of hunting in the big woods. The yearly bear hunt headed by General James Stone was probably the most cherished ritual of Faulkner's youth and early manhood. He makes its fictional version luminous for his reader. Seamlessly, the hunting story widens to engage the racial guilt that so often shadowed land-ownership in the 20th-century South. Such guilt was pervasive and speechless—concealed, so to speak, throughout the familiar surroundings—but if you wanted to find it, you could. It lodged in the commissary ledgers registering decades of black sharecroppers' misery—their endless indebtedness for white-dispensed food and clothing, and their inescapable indentured status. Those same ledgers went further back to the time of slavery before there were any black sharecroppers. The dusty pre-Civil War pages filled with dollars and cents intimated more broadly a 50-year history of white landowners buying and selling slaves. Pressed harder by Ike McCaslin, the commissary ledgers had yet more to reveal. Those 19th-century plantation masters—including Ike's own grandfather—did not only trade slaves. They also impregnated them, generation after generation. Reading past what the ledgers intended and finding what they didn't know they said, young Ike McCaslin discovered the full scandalous racial history of his family and his birthright. And he renounced them both in horror. The farm was not for him. He would instead become a landless hunter—"Uncle Ike," uncle to half a county and father to none. His fondest hope was to pass the rest of his days uncontaminated by his own family's unforgivable history.

It works—until "Delta Autumn," which serves as a sequel to "The Bear." This story follows the aged Ike attending, sometime in the 1940s, what is probably his last hunt. The wilderness has receded another 200 miles. A way of life is coming to an end. Yet, Ike remains ensconced in his memories, thinking "there was just exactly enough of it [the wilderness]" to last him out. And then comes the surprise: a woman, whom the younger men of the hunt have alluded to as the "doe," enters the campsite, approaching Ike's tent. A sullen Roth Edmonds (Ike's great-great-nephew) had given Ike an envelope for the woman the night before, with no explanations offered. Roth has no intention of seeing her himself; Ike is to hand her the envelope if she comes. The woman enters the tent, carrying an infant in her arms. She is Roth's mistress, and he is repudiating her, paying her off rather than acknowledging her. The money in the envelope Ike holds is for this purpose. As she talks to Ike, she reveals that she knows the entire history of his family. Of her own family, she mentions in passing that they used to take in washing:

> "Took in what?" he said. Took in washing?" He sprang, still seated even, flinging himself backward onto one arm, awry-

haired, glaring. Now he understood what it was she had brought into the tent with her. . . . the pale lips, the skin pallid and dead-looking yet not ill, the dark and tragic and foreknowing eyes. *Maybe in a thousand or two thousand years in America*, he thought. *But not now! Not now!* He cried, not loud, in a voice of amazement, pity, and outrage: "You're a nigger!" "Yes," she said. "James Beauchamp—you called him Tennie's Jim though he had a name—was my grandfather."

Maybe in a millennium or two, but not now... go slow now. The first act of miscegenation was initiated by Ike's grandfather 130 years earlier. Once again, it is being enacted by his great-nephew. Its consequence is embodied, six generations later, in the form of that sleeping infant. Ike cannot, at first, acknowledge the dark twin he sees in the mirror she provides. He urges her to go north and find a black man, anyone other than his great-nephew Roth. Her difference from his white line of descent is too great. "Took in washing:" from antebellum days through the Memphis garbage strike that cost Martin Luther King his life in 1968, black people have been cleaning up white people's dirt. And they have been treated like dirt because of it. Except that, even though Roth's lover cannot be like Ike, she carries his blood. Tennie's Jim—the miscegenous offspring of a long ago mating that was set up in the novel's opening story—did not disappear into oblivion. Over the subsequent decades, beyond narration, he sustained a name of his own, James Beauchamp, and a life of his own as well. Now he re-emerges into the narrative—at once the "doe's" grandfather and Ike's long lost (and disowned) black cousin. Even as Ike backs away in recoil, his hand reaches out to touch hers: "the gnarled, bloodless, bonelight bone-dry old man's fingers touching for a second the smooth young flesh where the strong old blood ran after its long lost journey back to home. 'Tennie's Jim,' he said. 'Tennie's Jim.'" The story of repudiation is also a story of family and love.

In his most compelling fictions of race, Faulkner recognized himself—uncomfortably, guiltily, responsibly—in the mirror of black distress at which he gazed. He was aware of his own role and knew that his entire life in the South entailed ineffaceable complicities. The solution to the race dilemma in America, should one ever be put into practice, would not be proposed by him. Rather than solutions, his work—at its best—would act as an unnerving dark twin intimating to its white reader: "Yes, you too are in this mirror, you will need to find a way to live with yourself insofar as you see yourself here." *Light in August, Absalom, Absalom!*, and *Go Down, Moses* constitute the most capacious mirror Faulkner was able to construct. It is not a magic mirror, and nothing we see reflected in it is likely to give much cause for satisfaction. But none of his white peers in the 20th century even attempted to see—and say—what he saw when he gazed into it.

Faulkner would write once again about racial turmoil. His last race-focused novel, *Intruder in the Dust*, appeared in 1948. Its keen (and easily decipherable) attention to contemporary racial agitation would doubtless play a part in his being awarded the Nobel Prize for Literature a year later. But that novel's stance was not just paternal—it was paternalistic as well. Its plot was simple: Lucas Beauchamp, now an old man charged with a murder he did not commit, had to be saved from lynching. Faulkner ensured that it would take white people working together to save Lucas. His efforts on his own behalf were to be quietly stymied (he remained locked up in jail). Thus, the motion and emotion in this novel belonged to the Southern whites who labored to clear an innocent black man. On one matter, Faulkner was crystal clear: Lucas's dilemma was not one in which well-meaning northern outsiders had any business interfering. Lucas's defense lawyer, Gavin Stevens, referred to his client as Sambo. One wonders how much is gained by freeing a black man only on the condition that he continues to answer to Sambo. Once again, looking forward and backward emerge as incoherently fused dimensions of Faulkner's racial imagination.

Intruder was commercially successful. Its first several weeks of sale outpaced even *Sanctuary's* record. MGM soon paid $50,000 for screen rights and then went on to fund the movie. Much of it was shot in Oxford during the spring of 1949. Faulkner helped the director, Clarence Brown, cast local acquaintances in several bit parts, and the world premiere took place in Oxford that fall. Regardless of personal opinions about Oxford's most celebrated resident, the town appreciated the business generated throughout several weeks of shooting. As the filming hullabaloo approached its end, Estelle decided that a fitting conclusion would be a party at Rowan Oak itself. There was, however, one hitch. A Puerto Rican named Juano Hernandez had been signed on to play the principal role in the story—that of Lucas Beauchamp. Faulkner had even helped Hernandez work on a black accent that would sound more like Mississippi than the Caribbean. Professional cooperation was one thing, but attendance at a Rowan Oak party was another. Hernandez himself was eminently presentable. But if they invited him, they would also have to invite his Negro hosts in Oxford. After some soul-searching, they determined they could not do that. So the whole crew, with the exception of the actor portraying the film's main character, came out to Rowan Oak. Whatever images Faulkner saw in the mirror posed by Juano Hernandez's black hosts, they did not figure for him as dark twins deserving acknowledgment.

5

Hollywood and Heartbreak

Faulkner's tempestuous Hollywood experience began in 1931. That December Sam Marx of MGM sent a telegram to his associate, Leland Hayward, which read: "DID YOU MENTION WILLIAM FAULKNER TO ME ON YOUR LAST TRIP UP HERE. IF SO IS HE AVAILABLE AND HOW MUCH." Faulkner had become too famous for the film studios to ignore him as a potential scriptwriter. He would bring to the one that hired him an invaluable cultural prestige, regardless of his talent for writing scripts. Marx's only question was how much it would cost to "buy" Faulkner. The price was $500 a week—a lot of money at the time. Without any illusions but also without much resistance, Faulkner signed up.

The extra money would come in handy. In 1929 after Faulkner married Estelle he quickly discovered that she liked expensive things; married life was not going to be cheap. In 1930, he purchased for the two of them (and their offspring-to-come) an antebellum Oxford home. He named it Rowan Oak, hoping the name might bring him the good luck associated with this tree, sacred in Scottish lore. The house was affordable (barely) only because it was badly in need of repair. Since Faulkner—ever a handy man—made many of these repairs himself, expenses were kept under control. But these savings were more than offset by his decision to include two black retainers, "Uncle" Ned Barnett and "Mammy" Caroline Barr, as members of his family retinue. He wanted to have children soon, so his family would, according to Southern customs, require the support of black helpers. As his only source of income was his writing and since he was prodigally irresponsible with money whenever it happened to come his way, Faulkner was chronically hard up for cash. So when MGM came calling, there was no way he could say no to the allure of Hollywood money. But that other Hollywood allure—the glamor of films and their larger-than-life stars—left Faulkner cold. He despised the celluloid medium and distrusted its moguls.

The country boy from Mississippi was a fish out of water during his frequent Hollywood stints. Los Angeles would remain for him an arid wasteland. As he once noted, "Nobody here does anything. There's nobody here with any roots. Even the houses are built out of mud and chicken wire." In real towns, people worked the land, producing and selling goods to other inhabitants; all of them had roots in the community. They came attached to parents, grandparents, uncles, aunts, and cousins; they had friends and enemies. This entire schema is saturated in widely disseminated stories. His own town, Oxford, was abuzz with what everyone might be doing, as well as lasting memories of what they might or might not have done in the past. As critic and literary scholar Hugh Kenner noted, Faulkner typically required three generations of family history in order to have a viable novel on his hands.

Faulkner's way of arriving in Hollywood suggests he was a misfit in Tinsel Town. He first appeared there on May 7, 1932, and, as he walked into Marx's office, he was bleeding from a head wound. He averred that, en route to Hollywood, he had been hit by a taxi in New Orleans. Marx told Faulkner his first job would be to work on a Wallace Beery picture. "Who's he?" Faulkner asked, before going on to tell Marx, "I've got an idea for Mickey Mouse." Marx explained that the famous mouse was a Disney property. Then he had an office boy take Faulkner to a projection room where a Beery film was being shown. Faulkner ignored the screen. Instead, he turned to the office boy and asked him if he owned a dog. The boy conceded he did not, to which Faulkner retorted, "Every boy should have a dog." He then berated the bewildered others in the room for not owning a dog. Although the Beery footage had barely gotten underway, Faulkner told the projectionist to turn it off. He said he already knew how the story would come out. Abruptly, he left MGM studios, reappearing nine days later looking shaky and obviously under the influence of booze. Asked to explain his absence, Faulkner said he had been wandering about in Death Valley. The entire vignette is telling: dogs mattered to him more than the film; Disney and MGM were for him interchangeable entities; a Beery film was boring because he knew in five minutes how it would turn out; he might or might not show up for work; his explanations made no sense; and he was obviously drinking. It was clear to Marx that Faulkner would never be a "company" man. Rattled by his behavior, Marx did not renew Faulkner's MGM contract the next month. Without the intervention of director, producer and screenwriter Howard Hawks, his Hollywood stint might have ended almost before it began.

Hawks would turn out to be the man who made Faulkner's 20-year-long Hollywood chapter viable. Hawks already knew and admired Faulkner's fiction. In 1932, he purchased film rights to "Turnabout," persuading the story's author to sign on as scriptwriter. Produced as *Today We Live*, this would be one of the few Faulkner scripts to make it to the screen. For the next two decades, Hawks played the role of Faulkner's guardian angel (if not his Faustian devil). He rehired Faulkner in 1934 for $1,000 a week to work on one of his screenplays. Later, he helped Faulkner secure a studio deal, which stipulated that he could work on Hollywood scripts while living at home in Oxford. No less, he brought Faulkner into the company of famous actors—Humphrey Bogart, Lauren Bacall, and Clark Gable, to mention just a few—who would become his drinking companions. Most fatefully, in 1935 Hawks introduced Faulkner to his own script girl, a charming Southern divorcee named Meta Carpenter.

Lonely, alienated by the money-frenzied Hollywood, and frustrated by a marriage that had gone rocky if not barren, Faulkner fell hard for Meta. By early 1936, he had persuaded her to become his lover. Their relationship remained largely concealed from the public until her memoir, *A Loving Gentleman*, appeared in 1976, 14 years after his death. The memoir emphasizes both Faulkner's courtliness and his passion. "Miss Meta," "m'honey," "dear one," and "ma'am" were the names he liked to call her. She became the idealized lover he had imagined Estelle to be back in 1918, a decade before he married her and his ideal collapsed. With Meta, he thought this dream was possible once more: "The idealization of me as a girl far too young for him was to last for a number of years," she wrote. "I never protested, and my acceptance of his vision of me as a maiden nourished his fantasy." There was pent-up sexual release as well. Soon, Faulkner was writing her tenderly obscene poems of gratitude: "For Meta, my heart, my jasmine garden, my April and May cunt; my white one, my blonde morning, winged, my sweetly dividing, my honey-cloyed, my sweet-assed gal. Bill." He showed her his unexpurgated copy of D. H. Lawrence's *Lady Chatterley's Lover*, and he developed for himself and Meta a set of kindred erotic phrases. Not *Chatterley's* "John Thomas" and "Lady Jane" for male and female genitalia, but rather "Mr. Bowen" and "Mrs. Bowen."

Close as they were, the two lovers were also distant. This may be how Faulkner wanted it or, at any rate, how (as with his own siblings) it simply had to be. His solitude was by now too deep-seated and impenetrable to be relinquished. Meta called him "a moated man" and "a great carapace." She would learn only long after his death that he had not actually flown in the Great War.

Notwithstanding their differences, what bonded Faulkner and Meta was a common vision for their future. They both wanted marriage, a second chance at love. Meta pressed to make it happen. "Let him go, Estelle," she thought (as she wrote in her memoir). "I can grow with him. You can't. I'm younger. Prettier. I can hold him, grace his life, keep him from alcohol, slake his passion, calm his volcanic rages." As for Faulkner, he seemed to recognize—before she did—that an affair in Hollywood was all they would ever successfully manage. He had inquired about divorce options when returning to Oxford in 1936, and he didn't like what he was told. Estelle would not only oppose him strenuously, but she would also keep him from his three-year-old daughter, Jill. Painfully, Faulkner and Meta had to readjust their sights. They tried to remain grateful for what they had: a love affair in a town famous for love affairs. It was difficult to imagine Meta in Oxford, what with his extensive world of family and acquaintances, shared memories and widespread stories. Privacy would prove impossible, and sociability even more so. The idyll would collapse of its own inappropriateness. Only in Hollywood, in rented rooms and on stolen occasions, was their passion viable at all. Later, she would reflect: he was "my lover, my rock; it was not enough, but I made it enough." For the next 15 years—though Meta would eventually marry another man (Wolfgang Rebner, a German pianist) and Faulkner would have other affairs—they remained true to each other, in their fashion.

The Rebners' marriage did not prosper. Faulkner's role in its failure is unknowable. The available evidence suggests that he never sought to intervene as Rebner's rival, nor did Rebner seem to resent Faulkner's prior place in his wife's affections. The decency with which all three seemed to treat each other over the next decade is remarkable. But Meta's off-and-on marriage allowed, at the same time, an intermittent relationship with Faulkner that was going nowhere. In 1939, weakened by an operation to remove a tumor and depressed by the failure of her marriage, she wrote Faulkner of her misery. She was heading home to her parents in Arizona to recuperate and to see if she could straighten her life out. He responded at once, urging her to route her train trip by way of Louisiana, where he would meet her. In a blinding rainstorm, he drove to the train junction and saw her emerge, feverish. They drove for hours through the storm to New Orleans and then checked into a hotel in the Vieux Carré. After a night of drinking and lovemaking, Meta awoke at noon, free of fever. Looking up in amazement, she saw Faulkner grinning at her as he answered her unstated question, "Good whiskey, and Mr. Bowen."

Meta returned from Arizona, determined to make her marriage work. But by 1942, she had filed for divorce. Again, she and Faulkner pursued their affair, but by now it clearly had no future. In 1945, she remarried Rebner, yet several years later—the marriage once more in ruins—she divorced him again. In the mid-1950s, a divorced and impoverished Meta found herself reduced to borrowing $150 from the now well-off (Nobel laureate) Faulkner. Having to do this filled her with shame. She sent him a check for $75 as soon as she could, promising the rest soon. He tore up the check, writing her back: "You can't possibly owe me anything like money; I remember too much."

Memory: this is perhaps the note to sound in closing a consideration of Faulkner and Meta Carpenter. He had sought in her a sanctuary to escape from the miseries of his life. He had many troubles: his marriage's failure, his California-imposed distance from his adored daughter, his ineffaceable guilt over Dean's death, and his discomfort at being caught in the money trap of Hollywood. Amid all the turmoil, Meta was like an illusion of transcendence. Together they would create an erotic utopia: just their two bodies and souls. Wonderful as it was—for a time—it could not be sustained. Nothing good, he came to believe, could be sustained. Alcohol soon found its way into their sanctuary. So did Estelle and Jill and Meta's husband, Rebner. Conceived as the opposite of normal life, their affair became, over time, caught up in normal life. "Between grief and nothing, I will take grief," Faulkner wrote to Meta in 1937. He would never have sought sanctuaries as aggressively as he did if he had not known that—lurking within them all—there would come the day of reckoning. The bell would sound, he would be in time again, and he would remember. There would be grief, and he would take it.

As Faulkner entered his 40s, his world was more out of control than ever before. Unpreparedness abidingly marked his life and work. But the appearance of Meta in 1935 had upped the ante and changed the equations. It can be no accident that his novel most marked by the besottedness of sexual passion—*If I Forget Thee, Jerusalem* (1938)—was written at this time. Rather than drawing on Meta's personality, it centers on the bodily phenomenon she unleashed in him: orgasmic discharge. Charlotte, one of the novel's two protagonists, is marked by "a faint inch-long scar on one cheek." She burns with unsmiling ferocity as she initiates Harry into the whirlpool of erotic consummation. The entire novel pivots on the unmanageable force of sexuality.

It is true that one-half of the novel ("Old Man")—insistently interwoven with the love-story half ("Wild Palms")—features no acts of intercourse. But no great leap of imagination is required to realize that the intercourse enacted literally in the love story of "Wild Palms" is enacted figuratively in the turbulent landscape of "Old Man." Faulkner was never to describe a more hallucinatory landscape than that of the ferocious Mississippi (the Old Man) flooding its borders (as it famously did in 1927). This cataclysm was uncontrollable, shedding a lurid light on all the puny manmade attempts meant to constrain its force. The protagonist of this narrative is an unnamed convict. He has been sent out into the water to rescue a stranded and terminally pregnant woman, equally unnamed. To accomplish this, he has only a frail boat between him and the exploding waters:

> [Suddenly the place] where the phosphorescent water met the darkness was now about ten feet higher than it had been an instant before and . . . it was curled forward upon itself like a sheet of dough being rolled out for a pudding. It reared, stooping; the crest of it swirled like the mane of a galloping horse. . . . He continued to paddle though the skiff had ceased to move forward at all but seemed to be hanging in space while the paddle still reached thrust recovered and reached again; now instead of space the skiff became abruptly surrounded by a welter of fleeing debris—planks, small buildings, the bodies of drowned yet antic animals, entire trees leaping and diving like porpoises above which the skiff seemed to hover in weightless and airy indecision like a bird above a fleeing countryside . . . while the convict squatted in it still going through the motions of paddling, waiting for an opportunity to scream. He never found it. For an instant the skiff seemed to stand erect on its stern and then . . .

Immersed in water like this, one does not steer. There is not even time to scream. The flow of time ceases and spatial demarcations vanish as well. Dry land with its orientational markers (trees, farms, roads) has morphed into a roiling universe of water. Horizontal becomes vertical, down becomes up, and forward becomes backward. Once-fixed things swirl by as moving and menacing debris. The sexual dynamic interior to "Wild Palms" figures here as outer apocalypse. The setting of this story has slipped its mapped and masculine fixity. All is now bottomless and unmanageable female waters. Fall into these and you drown. At their symbolic core—the targeted but unlocated object of the convict's quest—is a nine-months-pregnant woman. Excruciatingly swollen, she is on the verge of evacuating her own waters. The waterscape of "Old Man" keeps screaming the same message to the hapless convict: *you can't live here.* In this, it squarely intersects with the kindred message at the heart of the love story—one that Charlotte passes on to Harry: "You live *in* sin; you cant live on it."

Both stories circulate around something more primordial than fixed forms. Both center on liquid that has escaped its normal boundaries and is flowing uncontrollably. In the love story, that liquid is Charlotte's blood. The narrative opens in the perspective of a puritanical older doctor. He has been summoned to treat a badly—but invisibly—injured woman. Charlotte and Harry have rented the doctor's bungalow on the Gulf Coast. She is bleeding—fatally, it turns out—from Harry's botched abortion. Although the doctor senses immediately "the secret irreparable seeping of blood," his defenses keep him from knowing more. He has to ask, "Where is she bleeding?" and Harry responds, "Where do women bleed?"

Female bleeding had marked Faulkner's imagination long before this novel. In *The Sound and the Fury*, Quentin was mesmerized by women's menses. "Periodical filth between two moons balanced," so he fantasized a woman's monthly bleeding. *As I Lay Dying* and *Sanctuary* both attended hypnotically to an illicit rupture of the hymen. *Light in August* went on to consider more broadly this male obsession. Joe Christmas was terrified by where and why women bleed. When other boys first told him about menstruation, he rushed into the woods—in uncontainable distress—and sought out a stray sheep. He slaughtered it and then immersed his hands in its blood. He was seeking inoculation from the scandalous fact that the idealized object of male desire *leaks* every month. Joe thought he had procured such inoculation until—years later—he tried to have sex with the waitress Bobbie. Interrupting him, she murmured that she was having her period. Shocked speechless by the invisible liquid moving beneath her apparent stillness, he jabbed her hard twice in the head, then ran away at full speed. Soon he stopped within a grove of trees to catch his breath. All the trees seemed to him to be deformed and bleeding urns. Each was issuing, drop by drop, a deathly, foul-smelling liquid. Menstruation figures in Faulkner's imagination as an intolerable sign of instability and bodily rot—of "liquid putrefaction"—lurking within the female form.

But none of these earlier novels—no matter how intense their interest in female menses—centered on orgasm itself. And none of them drew so openly on recent personal experience. Here is Faulkner trying to say it to his editor Robert Haas in 1938: "To me, it [*If I Forget Thee*] was written just as if I had sat on the one side of a wall and the paper was on the other and my hand with the pen thrust through the wall and writing not only on invisible paper but in pitch darkness too." Here is Harry trying to say it in the novel proper: "Yes out of the terror in which you surrender volition, hope, all—the darkness, the falling . . . you yet feel all your life rush out of you into the pervading immemorial blind receptive matrix, the hot fluid blind foundation—grave-wound or womb-grave, it's all one." And here is the diagnosis offered by a doctor to the convict in "Old Man." (The convict has been bleeding through the nose for the entire narrative.) The doctor says, "Anyone ever suggest to you that you were hemophilic?"

Common to these three passages is the uncontrollable release of liquid. It pours through the pen, out the body, and from the nose. The release seems to occur "in pitch darkness" and its force is steeped in fatality: "grave-wound or womb-grave, it's all one." The bursting is ecstatic. It also overruns every boundary that makes selfhood recognizable. "Hemophilic:" the term suggests Faulkner's own prodigiously penetrable and "leaking" imagination. Things surge in and out of it too easily. Critics have long noted that vomiting plays a large role in Faulkner's fiction. It first shows up as the result of binges in the aviator stories. But in the greater work—*The Sound and the Fury* and *Light in August*—vomiting starts to signify more broadly the drama of the ego under assault, its incapacity to tolerate what is hurtling into it. In the suffocating presence of a black girl in a shed—this is to be his sexual initiation—the young Christmas explodes into violence. Her "black" smell has penetrated him, turned him topsy-turvy. He goes briefly berserk and tries to kill her.

"Hemophilic": Faulkner suffered from (and his work tapped unforgettably into) the overwhelming of his defenses. Eventually, he would learn that such bodily distress was—more deeply—synonymous with cultural distress. His hypersensitivity to the vertigo of "taking in" and "leaking out" made him a virtual seismographer of non-negotiable cultural encounters. Outrage—the signature event in his tragic work—is the overwhelming of culturally inculcated boundaries. Outraged and invaded, one is no longer oneself. Like Freud, Faulkner seems to have grasped that only what hurts is instructive. The lacerating wound carries the bad news that one's defenses have been breached, and one's inner boundaries have failed. His entire culture was fixated on mapping and maintaining differences between male and female, white and black, aristocrat and white trash. When these identity-sustaining boundaries collapsed, Faulkner registered with extraordinary power their fall-out: a sort of cultural hemorrhaging. What is the spectacle of light-skinned Joe Christmas parading in Mottstown's central square, waiting to be "recognized" as black, if not such a collapse? Miscegenation lies at the heart of both *Absalom, Absalom!* and *Go Down, Moses* (not to speak of Faulkner's own ancestral shadow family). What is this but the bursting—the hemorrhaging—of sanctuaries erected to keep out the unwanted other?

6

Alcohol and Accolades

G iven that life recurrently came at him in the form of outraging and overwhelming assault, Faulkner remained extraordinarily sensitive to the appeal of sanctuaries. These were rituals or practices whose repeatability might serve as protection or temporary escape. His sartorial extravagance—the military uniforms he wore after the Great War without being entitled to do so, the fox hunting regalia he later delighted in—speaks to this need for forms of predictable order. So, likewise, does the ceremonial two-week hunt in the Mississippi wilderness that he loved to embark on every autumn. Eventually, his failing health made the demanding wilderness trek inadvisable. He seemed to have found a satisfactory replacement in his later years, with the more sedate ceremony of Charlottesville fox hunting. A number of later photos show Faulkner in his magnificent hunting attire, sitting on his horse with silent dignity, every inch the Virginia aristocrat. (We don't know for sure but can suspect the irony he might have felt as the pomp-saturated pictures were being taken.)

Throughout his life, one sanctuary that never failed to fail him (to use his own phrasing in *Absalom, Absalom!*) was alcohol. Meta Carpenter had, at first, refused to believe Faulkner was a heavy drinker. In time, however, she would learn that his bond with the booze was more abiding than the one with her. He could not (and usually did not even try to) escape its hold. Like the other shaping forces in his life, the role of booze began long before his birth. His great-grandfather and grandfather were both well known as excessive drinkers. He remembered and retold (as though it were his own) a story about his grandfather, J. W. T. Falkner—successful citizen and president of Oxford's main bank. Deep in his cups one day, the old man lumbered into his big Buick (he owned the first car in Oxford), instructing his black driver to take him to the bank. Once there, J. W. T. clambered out of the car, picked up a good-sized brick, and hurled it into the bank's plate-glass window. Asked by wide-eyed bystanders why, he answered: "It's my Buick, my brick, and my bank." Throughout Faulkner's childhood, uncontrolled drinking was the stuff of colorful stories, a special precinct inhabited by his male ancestors. So it was no surprise that, by his late teens, he had become widely known as one of the town drunks.

At one level, alcoholism maintains its hold by way of chemical bondage. Psychology and culture cease to play a role at that level; the alcoholic cannot just will his way out of drinking. Yet, the drinker's personality—the values of his culture too—find their way into this picture as well. Southern boys typically learned to drink early—and hard—during their teens. It was a popular form of male camaraderie. The shared bottle was a talisman allowing them to secede from the world of womenfolk and adult responsibility—to declare once more their untamed independence. Later, in New Orleans in 1925 and surrounded by Sherwood Anderson's drinking companions, Faulkner widened his sense of alcohol's role in the emancipated life.

Further, from 1920 to 1933, there was the influence of Prohibition. Getting hold of liquor—always a fun activity for frisky boys—became doubly alluring when federal law meant that you might land in jail. There was a further risk that, since illicit booze was an uncontrolled and, therefore, potentially hazardous substance, it could seriously damage the drinker's health. A final contributing factor for Faulkner was the decades-long ritual of hunting in the Delta. This was a man's activity he had cherished ever since he was in his teens. Joining the annual hunting expedition in November led by General Stone (Phil Stone's father), Faulkner would confirm his sense of himself as a woodsman in the female-free company of like-minded men. Those two weeks in the big woods were lubricated by sustained nightly drinking. At these times, weighty memories and airy expectations would find their way into the ceremony of men-speech. As Faulkner put it in *Go Down, Moses*:

The best game of all, the best of all breathing and forever

the best of all listening, the voices quiet and weighty and
deliberate for retrospection and recollection and exactitude.
. . There was always a bottle present, so that it would seem to
him [the young Ike McCaslin] that those fine fierce instants
of heart and brain and courage and wiliness and speed were
concentrated and distilled into that brown liquor which not
women, not boys and children, but only hunters drank.

Although blessed with a resilient constitution, Faulkner drank to such
excess that, by his late 30s, he had serious health issues. His first
hospitalization for uncontrollable drinking, at Wright's Sanatorium in
Byhalia, Mississippi, occurred in June 1936. Twenty-six years later,
he was at Wright's again and suffered a fatal heart attack on July 6,
1962, one day after being admitted. In between, alcohol sent him
into the hospital dozens and dozens of times. Throughout the 1950s,
he was probably hospitalized every three months or so, though no
cures seemed to work for him. The therapies included the injection
of chemicals, electroshock, and psychoanalytic sessions; none of them
succeeded in separating Faulkner from the bottle. He seemed to have
believed, at the deepest level of his being, that he needed periodically
to drink himself into oblivion. It was his chosen way of shaking off
anxiety and stress, as a wet dog shakes off water. When younger, he
would typically come out of these binges refreshed and ready to return
to his commitments. It was as though he had drained the battery all the
way and could now recharge it effectively. But as he aged, the injuries
(to his body and mind) became graver. He eventually suffered from
convulsive seizures—so much so, that a Memphis doctor suggested a
spinal tap. Faulkner fled, as usual, to his Oxford retreat, Rowan Oak.
There he holed up, putting himself back together as best he could.

A final alcohol vignette remains. Faulkner's daughter Jill told this
one, culled from a reservoir of childhood memories, many of them
troubled. As one of her teenage birthdays approached, she noted
apprehensively that her father was moving toward a binge. She knew
what his binges were like: lasting from two days to more than a week,
they consisted of Faulkner sitting in his underwear in his bedroom,
well supplied with booze. There, he would consume bottle after bottle
until he decided he had had enough. Alarmed at this prospect, Jill

begged him to hold off the binge until after her birthday party. Hearing this plea once too often, he silenced her: "No one remembers Shakespeare's children." Perhaps, but Faulkner's child certainly remembered that zinger, and I heard her cite it in a TV interview some two decades later.

No single cause explains his alcoholism; rather, there were many contributing factors. A slew of unwanted thoughts and feelings that had accumulated in Faulkner's psyche over the years was likely at the heart of his drinking. From childhood on, he was hypersensitive and lonely. No less, there was the important role of the (male) Falkner tradition of excessive drinking: a self-damaging way of aligning himself with his ancestry. More broadly, there was probably the estranging vocation of letters in a Southern society that defined manhood otherwise. Then, there was guilt for the lies he told about his experiences in the Great War. (He had wanted badly to cut a bigger figure than he actually cut.) Sharpest of all, perhaps, was his guilt for the untimely death of his brother Dean, in Faulkner's own Waco. And in another key, there was cultural guilt (not felt by hordes of his compatriots) for his continued complicity in his region's abusive racial arrangements. More pervasively, there was guilt for having gotten himself into a troubled (and inescapable) marriage with a woman he either should have married earlier or (perhaps) not at all. Finally, there is likely to have been guilt for the messy love affairs that he pursued ardently—in his quest for some measure of the intimacy and erotic release lacking at home.

Drinking to numbness embodies—whatever else may be at play—a search for a sanctuary. It enacts a doomed attempt to forget who you are and how you came to be that way. Finally, though, who knows exactly why a man drinks himself to death? The stunning thing is not Faulkner's alcoholism per se—terrible though it was—but the fictional achievement he managed to craft despite it. After winning the Nobel Prize for Literature in 1949, Faulkner would rarely again encounter money troubles. Nor would there be major hurdles to getting his work published. But the period that tells most about his character occurred two decades earlier. This was the time when he struggled to market his stories and novels, tirelessly and against unremitting odds. Throughout these years, the editors kept turning him down. Unvanquished, he kept sending his work out. (He later advised a would-be writer that until his stuff had been turned down a hundred times, he hadn't yet gotten to zero.) Regardless of the array of reasons for beating Faulkner down, he just would not quit. As his beleaguered Jack Houston thinks (in *The Hamlet*), "I dont understand it. I dont know why. I wont ever know why. But You cant beat me. I am strong as You are. You cant beat me."

Though the inner troubles he suffered from were never resolved, eventually fame did come. Its first onslaught had occurred in the early 1930s. After the lightning-like publication of *The Sound and the Fury, As I Lay Dying, Sanctuary,* and *Light in August* in just three years—a pace of masterpieces matched only by Shakespeare—Faulkner had become impossible to ignore. The New York literati were all over him. Soon he established what would be a lifelong commitment to Random House as his chosen press. In 1949—having published 13 novels, half of them supremely good—Faulkner finally won the big prize, the Nobel. Not without anxiety had the Nobel judges agreed to bestow their award on him. And not without strategic skirmishing was he persuaded to go to Stockholm to make his acceptance speech. His 17-year-old daughter Jill accompanied him. The pedagogic argument that she would benefit from exposure to European culture was cunningly deployed as leverage to get him there.

His need for privacy was inveterate, however, and arguments of the sort deployed by the Nobel Committee usually failed to persuade him. He would later even decline an invitation to the Kennedy White House. Although by then he lived in Charlottesville—to be nearer to his daughter and grandchildren—the 100-mile trip to Washington was "a long way to go just to eat." To the end, he preferred calling himself not a writer but a farmer. More, he never advised other writers how to improve their craft. No one, he believed, had ever taught him much about improving his own. Such reticence marked him early and late in life, surely contributing to the stresses in his marriage with a vibrant and sociable Southern woman like Estelle. No less, it kept him on the far side of the various ceremonies associated with literary success. To him, participation in professorial conferences where practitioners of letters joined literary scholars to share anecdotes and insights would have been torture. He never went past the 11th grade and—genius though he was—he had nothing to teach the professors. And he was sure he had even less to learn from them.

Throughout the 1950s—a decade that saw the publication of four of his last five novels—Faulkner was a famous man. Steadily he was receiving accolades. *A Fable*—uniquely recalcitrant and long in gestation (he struggled with it throughout much of the 1940s)—finally appeared in 1954. It won the Pulitzer Prize the following year. It was too big an effort to ignore, yet it was also too difficult to read—too overwritten and portentous—to gain a readership. Of the various reasons that shed light on its failure to gain traction with the public, two are especially salient. The first is that Faulkner was off his native turf. The bulk of *A Fable* takes place not in Yoknapatawpha County but on the battlefields of France, during the Great War of 1914-1918. Its theme is crystalline: the absurdity of that war. Thus, it launches a Christ-like attempt by the "Corporal" to foment a cease-fire that would, if sufficiently widespread, shut down the entire war. But the powers that be—represented by the "General"—are not about to let the cease-fire succeed. The narrative moves steadily toward the crucifixion—literally the court-martial-mandated execution of the Corporal—wrought into the book's allegorical premises. Corporal and General/ Christ and God/crucifixion: the Christian frame is blatant, perhaps suffocating. The rhythms of Yoknapatawpha County—with its characters, plots, landscape, anecdotes, and humor—are rarely near.

The second reason that *A Fable* is broadly judged a failure has to do with Faulkner's prose for writing it. Studded with orotund sentences that seem to go on forever, *A Fable* tends to wear out its reader. (It is mainly professional "Faulknerians" who argue for the book's importance.) Here we touch on a besetting condition of Faulkner's work when it fails its own standards. The name I bestow upon this condition is "Faulknerese." Any reader of this book who has previously failed to make it through the forest of Faulknerese may have an idea of what I'm talking about. For that reason, it is worth characterizing further this turgid territory.

"Faulknerese" is a verbal practice committed to proliferating syntax and Latinate/polysyllabic vocabulary. Its insistence manifests itself in sentence after sentence that thunders onward. "Faulknerese" does not select or pare down, and it has little interest in the single, telling detail or in pausing and letting the reader catch his breath. "Faulknerese"—either previously encountered or dreaded in advance—is a major reason many readers are skittish toward Faulkner's work. Let's see how it operates in *A Fable*. I cite the arrival (a few pages into the book) of a speeding military car carrying the three top generals. They have come to crush the incipient rebellion:

> It [the car] came fast, so fast that the shouts of the section leaders and the clash of rifles as each section presented arms and then clashed back to 'at ease', were not only continuous but overlapping, so that the car seemed to progress on one prolonged crash of iron as on invisible wings with steel feathers,—a long, dusty open car painted like a destroyer and flying the pennon of the supreme commander of all the allied armies, the three generals sitting side by side in the tonneau amid a rigid glitter of aides,—the three old men who held individual command over each of the three individual armies, and the one of that three who, by mutual consent and accord, held supreme command over all (and, by that token and right, over everything beneath and on and above the distracted half-continent)—the Briton, the American, and between them the Generalissimo: the slight gray man with a face wise, intelligent, and unbelieving, who no longer believed in anything but his disillusion and his intelligence and his limitless power—flashing across that terrified and aghast amazement and then gone, as the section leaders shouted again and the boots and the rifles crashed back to simple alert.

This is a carefully meditated piece of writing, yet its unrelenting grandiloquence makes it hard to come to terms with. A slew of words is being hurled, torrentially, at the reader. Earlier, to be sure, I claimed that Faulkner's difficulty was inseparable from his achievement. The opening pages of *Absalom, Absalom!* are even more daunting than this passage. (You may remember my mentioning that my first reading of *Absalom* ended with throwing the book down in disgust.) But a necessary difficulty is a far cry from a gratuitous one. *Absalom's* difficulty—like that of Faulkner's other earlier masterpieces—tests a reader's willingness to sustain confusion by not knowing enough in time. This is a necessary difficulty—necessary because all throughout our lives we suffer from such not-knowing-yet. Whatever light Faulkner can shine on it is precious.

The difficulty of the passage from *A Fable* has nothing to do with our not knowing enough in present time—our unpreparedness for what is at stake in a moment of experience. Instead, the passage is static—a monumental tableau—as it presses us to attend to the stature of its cast of officers. The prose claims that the Generalissimo's "supreme command" extends to everything "beneath and on and above the distracted half-continent." That quoted phrase is slack, as are "by mutual consent and accord," "by that token and right," and "terrified and aghast amazement." We are in the presence of a "big" scene full of bombastic phrases—a scene where the author pulls out the stops to make sure we register how big it is. To put it simply, the prose engages in overkill. Unfortunately, the two novels that precede *A Fable—Intruder in the Dust* (1948) and *Requiem for a Nun* (1951)—often rely on the same heavy linguistic artillery. They labor hard to impress us. Since it is distasteful to dwell on a writer's weaknesses, I will now move to other matters. But there is one caveat: the Faulkner who matters throughout this study—the *great* Faulkner—does not write Faulknerese.

In 1951, Faulkner won the National Book Award for his *Collected Stories*. Four years later, *A Fable* garnered that prize as well. "Collected": the term is resonant. Throughout the 1940s and 1950s, Faulkner sought to "collect"—to bring together and make good on—a range of creative enterprises launched earlier. Addie Bundren (in *As I Lay Dying*) speaks of the need to clean up the house before leaving it, and Faulkner was cleaning up his literary house. As early as 1925, he had conceived his major "white trash" fictional family—the ever-reproducing Snopeses—and he returned to them only in 1940.

That is the year when *The Hamlet* appeared, releasing the

unflappable Flem Snopes onto his fictional canvas. By way of the Compsons and Sartorises (major figures in a number of his early novels), Faulkner already had his say about doomed Southern aristocracy. He had shown how their world of pre-Civil-War values left them helpless in the face of post-Civil-War realities. The Snopeses, by contrast, allowed him to see what no Compson or Sartoris's lens could encompass. Through them (and their number is legion) he explored the options and intricacies operative in the New South. This was a South long departed from Civil War exploits and catastrophes, unburdened by that War's trauma and fallout. Indeed, *The Hamlet* is one of Faulkner's most capacious novels and deserves more than the passing attention this brief study can give it. It is also his most conventional masterpiece. Readers who dislike Faulkner's work, in general, tend to make an exception for *The Hamlet*. Like *If I Forget Thee, Jerusalem*, it attends powerfully to the madness of love. No less, though, it offers Faulkner's most extensive take on the changes in economic structure and ideological stance occurring in the South in the mid-20th century. Its teeming cast of characters manifestly had more to give Faulkner, but it would take 17 more years before he could take up their offer. The second volume of the Snopes trilogy, *The Town*, appeared only in 1957. Now that he had a head of steam, the last volume, *The Mansion*, progressed swiftly, coming out just two years later.

In the same vein of "collecting" and cleaning up, *Intruder in the Dust* (1948) completed the racial stories launched in *Go Down, Moses* (1942). The same black protagonist, Lucas Beauchamp, is central to both novels. No less, *Requiem for a Nun* (1951) reprises the unruly story of Temple Drake that Faulkner had broached in *Sanctuary* (1931). (That earlier scandalous novel would have struck him as a case for "cleaning up," if ever there was one.) All told—apart from *A Fable*—every novel Faulkner wrote during these two decades enacts a form of creative house-cleaning. Departure was on his mind, and he was working out his leave-taking. Faulkner's last novel, *The Reivers* (1962), also won the Pulitzer Prize. It unfolds as a bucolic goodbye to his entire teeming world—reprising many earlier characters and locales. But this time, he reprises them in the form of romance rather than tragedy. "Pappy" (as Faulkner's grandchildren fondly called him) had taken over the creative pen. The opening phrase of *The Reivers* is "Grandfather said." Nothing terrifying was going to happen on its fit-for-children, nostalgic pages.

A commitment to "cleaning up" spurred not only Faulkner's creative output, but also his social engagement. Throughout the 1950s, after he won the Nobel Prize, institutions of American culture and diplomacy solicited his support. There was a new kind of war going on, the Cold War, and a new enemy, Russian communism. The State Department found (perhaps to its surprise) that Faulkner was serviceable. With a modicum of careful handling, this unpredictable genius could perform as an effective spokesman for US values. He traveled for the State Department to South America and Japan, where he carried out his tasks with unfailing generosity and civility.

At home in America, the need for "cleaning up" had also become dramatic. Civil rights turmoil, simmering anew since the return of black soldiers in 1945, was erupting into crisis. Awkwardly yet movingly, Faulkner rose to its challenge. At some personal risk, he sought to moderate the violence and to identify common ground between the races. His family knew he did not want to live with blacks, and they despised his publicly pretending that he did. But they were wrong in this judgment. Faulkner did not want to live with blacks personally, but to help America figure out how to live with them nationally. The issue was clear: how to confront the fallout from the country's foundational trauma—slavery—and turn it toward a civil future. Whatever else his travels around the world taught him, they taught him that racial equality was the only possible stance America could endorse in the contemporary world.

It is tempting to conclude this brief study of Faulkner on the note of "cleaning up." As readers, and human beings, we want to see problems worked through, or, at least, to understand them at last. We want the passage of time to turn confusion into insight, messiness into cleanliness, storm into calm. But Faulkner's deepest bid on our attention—as I suggested in my introductory remarks about why we cannot have a "simple Faulkner"—requires a change in our expectations. Resolution, he came to see, is an aesthetic requirement (the work must have form). But it is rarely a life reality. Yet, most Western fiction before the great 20th-century modernists—not only Faulkner, but also Marcel Proust, James Joyce, Franz Kafka, and Virginia Woolf, among others—chose to write plotted stories rather than attempt a narration of unplotted life. Beginning with *The Sound and the Fury*, Faulkner (like his modernist peers) went the other way. Once he took that plunge, his work forsook forever the seductions attaching to "simple."

Instead of "simple" he took on—and worked brilliantly to get his reader to take on—something rarer and more precious. He got us to encounter life as it outrageously erupts before we master it and convert it into familiar narrative patterns. Faulkner's freshness and power lodge here. When caught up in present turmoil, when called to act before we know how to act, we are not knowing, authoritative beings. We are not the writers of our script, but—suddenly—players stumbling through a drama written not by us but by conditions over which we have little control. We are caught up in a pervasive and impersonal storm—one that is culturally shaped, decades if not centuries in the making.

To write the drama of the human being under such stress—rather than to tell tidy stories—Faulkner had to wrench his fiction free from the blandishments of satisfying plot-resolution. He had to learn to write sound and fury. That he did so with such power suggests that the stumbling that vexed his life also served as an inexhaustible quarry for his fiction. I close by citing again the words of reviewer Evelyn Scott, as she responded to the manuscript of *The Sound and the Fury* in 1929. She understood what Faulkner had wrought: "Here is beauty sprung from the perfect *realization* of what a more limiting morality would describe as ugliness. Here is a humanity stripped of most of what was claimed for it by the Victorians, and the spectacle is moving as no sugar-coated drama ever could be." It is the spectacle of being off-balance and lurching, of being seen and respected and pitied as we moved through the stages of our fall, heading toward the earth. "The human heart in conflict with itself": so Faulkner identified (in his Nobel Prize acceptance speech) his core concern. He took this conflict too seriously to console or pretend to resolve. His work, like his life, was rarely about succeeding, and not often about prevailing. Both the life and the work served, instead, as luminous testimony to engaging and enduring life's assault. *That* is the drama he passed on to his readers.

Suggested Reading

For a deeper understanding of Faulkner—his work and its impact—nothing is more productive than to read his fiction itself. (Faulkner himself was adamant on this point. He once directed his critics to the obituary comment about himself that he would most endorse: "He made the books, and he died.") This study has sought to introduce the reader to his major works. The best next step is to engage them personally, by plunging in.

Many excellent commentaries light the way to such an undertaking. As I mentioned in my study, several illustrious French thinkers of the early 20th century—Malraux, Sartre, and Camus, among them—were fascinated by Faulkner as early as the 1930s. Their commentary (in the form of essays or introductions) is still capable of startling the 21st-century reader with its brilliance.

Faulkner taught a course in creative writing at the University of Virginia in 1957-1958. There he became friendly with an enterprising assistant professor, Joseph Blotner, whom he eventually appointed as his official biographer. Blotner's magisterial *Faulkner: A Biography* appeared in a two-volume edition in 1974. Ten years later, Blotner brought out a one-volume edition. It immediately became—and still is—our best introduction to Faulkner's life. Blotner knew Faulkner personally, having maintained a convivial relationship with the writer during the last five years of his life—which was not possible for later biographers.

Faulkner's privileged position in American culture was perhaps at its peak between 1960 and 1990. Innumerable first-rate commentaries were written about him during those decades. If you were a college student studying literature in the United States at that time, it would have been hard to avoid one or more of his novels on your course syllabi. Beginning in 1974, the University of Mississippi launched its Faulkner and Yoknapatawpha series of conferences. As of the date of this writing—May 2016—that yearly conference remains vibrant. Its organizers invite scholars from all over the world to come and deliver their thoughts about Faulkner. These essays are later revised and published as part of the Faulkner and Yoknapatawpha series. I urge any reader curious to explore further dimensions of Faulkner's work to consult the volumes in this series. Its range is exemplarily large.

Beyond this, I might sketch out the following critical pathway through the commentary on Faulkner. Drawing on Nietzsche and Freud, John Irwin's *Doubling and Incest / Repetition and Revenge* (1976) opened the way for the study of a more theoretical and philosophical Faulkner. In the next decade, John T. Matthews's *The Play of Faulkner's Language* (1982) and Eric Sundquist's *Faulkner: The House Divided* (1983) further enlarged the domain of scholarship devoted to Faulkner, subjecting him to a deconstructive lens (Matthews) and examining more thoroughly his grasp of racial dynamics (Sundquist). To this pair of American authors, one should add a trio of sophisticated French critics whose work has been devoted extensively to Faulkner: André Bleikasten, Michel Gresset, and François Pitavy. Bleikasten's role has been especially influential. His *The Ink of Melancholy* (1990) provides an authoritative analysis of Faulkner's early masterpieces. All of these writers have continued to write about Faulkner.

My own work on Faulkner first appeared in the 1990s; *Becoming Faulkner* (2009)—attentive to both his life and his art—is the third book I have devoted (entirely or in part) to this writer. Noel Polk's *Children of the Dark House* (1998) showcases Polk's textual expertise (he was in charge of most modern editions of Faulkner's novels). In addition, Joel Williamson's *Faulkner and Southern History* (1993) and Don Doyle's *Faulkner's County: The Historical Roots of Yoknapatawpha* (2001) provide indispensable historical background for understanding Faulkner's fiction.

Anthologies of work devoted to Faulkner continue unabated. Among others, my *The Cambridge Companion to William Faulkner* (1995) contains useful essays that open up Faulkner's world. Matthews has just edited *The New Cambridge Companion to William Faulkner* (2015), as well as *William Faulkner in Context* (2015), in which the widest range of contemporary approaches to this writer is on display. Readers interested in learning more about Faulkner have only to turn to some of this work—published earlier or appearing now—to extend their horizons.

About the Author

Philip Weinstein taught at Harvard University and later at Swarthmore College where, since 1990, he has been Alexander Griswold Cummins Professor of English. Past president of the William Faulkner Society (2000-2003), he has written (or edited) four books on Faulkner: *Faulkner's Subject: A Cosmos No One Owns* (1992), *The Cambridge Companion to William Faulkner* (1995), *What Else But Love? The Ordeal of Race in Faulkner and Morrison* (1996), and *Becoming Faulkner*(2010), which won the 2010 Hugh Holman Award as the best book on Southern culture. In addition to his work on Faulkner, Weinstein has published widely on modern European fiction.

Afterword

Thank you for reading *Simply Faulkner*!

If you enjoyed reading it, we would be grateful if you could help others discover and enjoy it too.

Please review it with your favorite book provider such as Amazon, BN, Kobo, iBooks or Goodreads, among others.

Again, thank you for your support and we look forward to offering you more great reads in the future.

A Note on the Type

Cardo is an Old Style font specifically designed for the needs of classicists, Biblical scholars, medievalists, and linguists. Created by David J. Perry, it was inspired by a typeface cut for the Renaissance printer Aldus Manutius that he first used to print Pietro Bembo's book *De Aetna*, which has been revived in modern times under several names.